PUBLIC PHILOSOPHY SOCIETY

Journal of Public Philosophy

Volume 1 Issue 1

Public Philosophy Press

First published by Public Philosophy Press 2019

Copyright © 2019 by Journal of Public Philosophy

General Editor, Kelly Fitzsimmons Burton

Cover art by Beth Ellen Nagle

First edition

We dedicate this collaborative effort to our esteemed colleague and friend,
Dr. Rodney W. Tussing (1949 - 2019)

Contents

Preface

The *Journal of Public Philosophy* is the official publication of the Public Philosophy Society. The goal of the *Journal* is to publish papers, essays, and book reviews in the mode of classical philosophy. We seek to know the basic truths that are foundational for the common good, and a just and civil society.

The goal of public philosophy is to make the practice of philosophy more accessible and more relevant to students, scholars, and the broadly educated public. We hope to inspire young and old alike in the shared, rational pursuit of wisdom and in love of Being, Unity, the True, the Good, and the Beautiful.

Public philosophy is inspired by Socrates' engagement in dialogue in the agora, the shared public space of the city-state. It is the pursuit of the common good, our shared life together. Currently, we are a group of professors seeking to bring the discussions usually reserved for the classroom into a broader context. We hope that others will join us in an ever-broadening and deepening discussion. The arena for discussions has been college and university public lecture forums, book discussion groups, and campus clubs. We hope that others will expand the public context, perhaps meeting at coffee shops and houses of worship. We have expanded the discussion to an international group with the formation of the Public Philosophy Society.

The Public Philosophy Society is a professional society, offering membership to students, scholars, and educated members of the public. For more information about joining the Society, visit our membership site: https://www.patreon.com/pubphisociety .

The *Journal of Public Philosophy* welcomes submissions for publication by scholars and practitioners in Public Philosophy who share this vision. Submissions may be sent to: info@publicphilosophypress.com

The *Journal of Public Philosophy* is published by Public Philosophy Press: www.publicphilosophypress.com

Kelly Fitzsimmons Burton, General Editor

Contributors

Owen Anderson, Ph. D. is Professor of Philosophy and Religious Studies in the New College at Arizona State University. In 2013-2014 he was the William E. Simon research fellow in the James Madison Program at Princeton University and a visiting scholar at Princeton Seminary. He has published seven books including *The Declaration of Independence and God* (Cambridge University Press, 2015) and *The Natural Moral Law* (Cambridge University Press, 2013).

Kelly Fitzsimmons Burton, Ph. D. is a professor of Philosophy and Religious Studies at Paradise Valley Community College in Phoenix, AZ. She is the author of *Retrieving Knowledge: A Socratic Response to Skepticism* (Public Philosophy Press, 2018) and *Reason and Proper Function: A Response to Alvin Plantinga* (Public Philosophy Press, 2019).

Surrendra Gangadean, Ph. D, is Emeritus Professor of Philosophy and Religious Studies at Paradise Valley Community College in Phoenix, AZ. He is the author of *Philosophical Foundation: A Critical Analysis of Basic Belief* (University Press of America, 2009).

Arturo Gastelum is a Ph. D. student in Humanities with an emphasis in Philosophy at Faulkner University. His research interest is in the relationship between faith and reason.

Mevin Joshi is Instructor of Philosophy and Religion at Arizona State University and Founder and Chairman of Clarity Fund, Inc. (clarityfund.org).

Peter A. Redpath, Ph. D. is retired Full Professor of Philosophy at St. John's University, New York, and is CEO of the Aquinas School of Leadership, Rector of the Adler-Aquinas Institute and Senior Fellow at the Center for the Study of The Great Ideas. He is author of twelve philosophical books [including *The Moral Psychology of St. Thomas Aquinas: An Introduction to Ragamuffin Ethics* (En Route Books & Media, 2017), *A Not-So-Elementary Christian Metaphysics*, Vol. 2 (En Route Books & Media, 2016), and *A Not-So-Elementary Christian Metaphysics*, Vol. 1 (En Route Books & Media, 2nd printing, 2015] and numerous articles and book reviews.

Rodney W. Tussing, Ph. D. taught Philosophy and Religious Studies at Arizona State University, Grand Canyon University, and Paradise Valley Community College. He is the author of *Religion and Science: Deconstructing a Modern Paradigm* (Public Philosophy Press, 2019).

In Memoriam

Rod Tussing (1949-2019) - A Good and Faithful Witness

I was privileged to witness Rod Tussing's life, from his conversion to his departure. Conversion began in philosophy class and came to confession of faith, while together, uniquely, the first.

He grew in understanding and affirmed a constant faith in all of life. He was a husband and father, yet his family became all who hear the Word of God and put it into practice.

In the course of time he came to supervise hundreds in constructing a building for technology that serves millions. His artistic sensibility showed itself in the art of painting and in the nuances of wood staining.

By faith, he engaged with academic challenges in philosophy and religion, against skepticism and fideism. His M.A. thesis (*Religion and Science: Deconstructing a Modern Paradigm*, 2019) and his Ph.D. dissertation (Forthcoming by *his* request, 2020) are published by Public Philosophy Press. His lectures and talks continue in the hearts of many, and continue to speak from(TheLogosPaideia.org). He was a team player, a friend, and a colleague, who longed for the fullness of life in the City of God.

He fought the good fight for the good; he finished *his* portion of the race; and, in the face of the final suffering, he kept the faith. He now has joined the great, invisible company of witnesses who have gone before us, who are waiting, watching, and wishing for the completion of the work given to mankind.

Surrendra Gangadean—mentor and friend

Common Ground for Public Discourse

Surrendra Gangadean, Ph. D.

Public discourse has collapsed in the recent culture wars. It is a predictable stage in the unfolding culture of every civilization that allows some freedom of thought. Freedom of thought apart from the laws of thought spins out of control. "Things fall apart; the center cannot hold; Mere anarchy is loosed upon the world . . ." Can we have freedom without anarchy? Can there be rule by consent? We can and must have freedom and consent if we are to have any civilization, that is to say, a full common life, that is the say, *human* life, life that is beyond the birds and bees and beasts. Common life requires common ground. And common ground is to be found in human nature itself, understood more consciously and consistently.

Common Ground, in its most basic sense, is the set of conditions that make thought and discourse possible. The set unfolds naturally from the most basic, logically and objectively, to the existentially and subjectively basic; from the method of knowledge to the content of knowledge, all beginning, as it should, at the most basic level of our being. Common ground consists of reason as the laws of thought which make thought and discourse (the sharing of thought for consent) possible. This is not a mere professed but actual commitment to the use of reason, a concern for consistency in thought and action, which is integrity. Applied consistently, reason is used critically to first test one's own basic belief for meaning. Reason, testing basic beliefs, is rational presuppositionalism (RP). Reason, Integrity and RP

1

lead to the Principle of Clarity (PC): somethings are clear; the basic things are clear; the basic things in metaphysics (about God and man), and in ethics (about good and evil) are clear to reason (epistemology). Common Ground *must* begin with and build upon what is self-evident in epistemology.

It is self-evident that we think: we form concepts, judgments and arguments, the forms of all thought, from the most basic concepts express by a word or a term, to judgment relating two concepts, to argument the most complex thought, drawing a conclusion from premises. Thinking is cognitive, requiring judgments that are true or false, and concepts which distinguish things, a and not a. It is also self-evident that there are laws of thought: identity—a is a; non-contradiction—not both a and not-a at the same time and in the same respect; excluded middle—either a or not-a. These laws of thought are properly called the laws of reason, or *reason-in-itself*, to distinguish it from other, less basic senses of the term 'reason'.

From these two self-evident truths—that we think, and there are laws of thought— several other thoughts follow. Reason as the laws of thought is the test for meaning. Reason as the laws of thought make thought possible. What violates a law of reason cannot be thought. A *is* not-a (fish *is* not-fish) cannot be thought. The words in the utterance become meaningless, emptied of meaning, when joined together. Since truth requires meaning, loss of meaning brings the loss of truth. Reason is authoritative *because* it is transcendental—the laws of thought make thought possible. It therefore cannot be questioned without becoming self-referentially absurd. Only reason, *as* the laws of thought, is self-attesting. One can be free to think (to form concepts etc.) only by observing the laws of thought, that is, the laws of reason.

By nature, we think, even as we breathe; it cannot be prevented. It is common to all human beings *as humans*, regardless of other differences (age, gender, race, culture). We have bodies also, as animals, and sense experience. But a sense (bodily) impression, which is particular, is not a concept, which is universal. This distinguishes reason from the senses, thinking from perceiving, mind from body, man from animal. Because reason is natural, in our nature, it is universal, the same in all who think, and therefore reason *is* common ground.

Reason does not apply only to thought but also to being. There are no square-circles, no a that is not-a. What is logically impossible is ontologically impossible; it cannot exist in any possible world. So, there are no uncaused events, no being from non-being. Reason applies to *all* being, to the highest being, to God's being (God is not both eternal and not-eternal in the same respect at the same time). Reason is eternal and uncreated. Miracles may override a created law of nature but cannot override reason. Reason gives certainty, not just about relations among ideas, but in metaphysics also, about the world, about what is or can be eternal.

Reason in man is fundamental to desire (what we view as a good) and to action (what we choose to do in pursuit of the good). Since *no* experience (ordinary *or* extraordinary) is meaningful without interpretation, reason is fundamental (to the meaning of experience and to the meaning of truth statements). The psychological and the practical presupposes cognitive/rational meaning. Meaning is the deepest need and the highest good for man as a rational being, and therefore the source of man's greatest happiness. Its absence is the source of man's deepest misery.

No area of life is exempt from thought and no thought is exempt from meaning and therefore from reason. There is no *religious* exemption from reason. Faith is to reason as truth is to meaning. The deeper the understanding of what is not visible, the deeper is one's faith. Reason therefore is the *beginning* of common ground for all human beings, in all of life.

Integrity is a concern for consistency, both logical and existential. Without consistency, thought and dialogue become absurd/futile. Moral evil is an act contrary to one's nature as a human being. It is to neglect, avoid, resist and deny reason regarding what is clear. Suffering calls us to stop and think. As humans, under the condition of natural and moral evil, we are more less conscious and consistent. And all agree we should be more conscious and consistent—we all should have integrity.

With integrity, we would seek and understand basic things that are clear to reason. We would come to agreement and grow in that agreement about what is clear. Either nothing (or not much) is clear, or, we generally lack integrity in not seeking and not understanding. But no one, psychologically, can easily admit to lack of integrity. Concern for truth is so inward and compelling that a special kind of self-blinding (hypocrisy) is necessary to avoid what is clear. Hypocrisy can be maintained only by a continual hardening of oneself by self-justification in order to excuse oneself from a sense of guilt in not seeking and understanding.

Recognizing the propensity to hypocrisy requires the humility to be open to correction through self-examination. Dialogue recognizes historically cumulated insight in others. Fear of human suffering should spur self-examination. Challenges of different views calls for thoughtful dialogue. We should seek out authority based on insight in order to be challenged.

In light of reason and clarity at the basic level, integrity through self-examination is necessary and sufficient for knowledge. What is clear, and *all* that is clear, beginning with the self-evident and a building on that, is easily knowable, with integrity. Integrity is necessary as common ground. Without integrity, we cannot get off the ground.

Critical thinking applies reason as the test for meeting, first at the basic level, and first in one's *own* basic beliefs (presuppositions). Reason used to test presupposition for meaning is called rational presupposition (RP). RP is simply critical thinking applied more consciously and consistently. RP differs from other epistemologies by being alert to uncritically held assumptions and by attempting to be more conscious and consistent in critical thinking at the foundational level.

There are two sets of basic beliefs in the three areas of basic beliefs.

How do I know? (epistemology): either somethings are clear or nothing is clear. What is real/eternal? (metaphysics): either all is eternal (in some form or other) or only some is eternal. What ought I to do? (ethics): either the good (the end in itself) is clear (because it is based on human nature which is rational) or the good is not clear (because there is no rational human nature). In these three basic questions, ethics (the good) is based in metaphysics (human nature), the understanding of which is grounded in epistemology. We must begin with *epistemology*.

RP presupposes integrity and integrity presupposes what is self-evident: that we think and that there are laws of thought—reason in itself. But no one is fully conscious and consistent in their presuppositions, given the factors of personality, background and mood. Each person and every group of persons have an admixture of both sets of basic beliefs held more or less consciously and consistently, with one set being more basic (at any time, from time to time, and over time). History is the outworking of the conflict of basic beliefs in each person and in every group of persons. Being contradictory, only one set can be true; only one set retains meaning. RP both intensifies and resolves conflicts and bring things to a head—by making clear what is meaningful.

RP is to be contrasted with other epistemologies. Tradition is the default position of most human beings and is transmitted by testimony (teaching of the elders). Scripture is passed on by testimony, but RP asks why any scripture, why is this scripture and why this scripture rather than another? When reasons are given without critical thinking they are not rationally relevant. They are pseudo-arguments, not arguments; they appeal to the psychological and the practical, not the rational.

After tradition, common sense may be appealed to (a form of hoary tradition) as well as appeal to numbers also. Common sense is a form of naïve realism, which takes appearance for reality, a quasi-pragmatism that shifts the burden of proof to the opposing party. A less sophisticated form is Thomas Reid's Scottish Common Sense philosophy. A more sophisticated form is Plantinga's Reformed Epistemology which focuses on warrant, which may be lost, not on rational justification testing basic beliefs for meaning, which cannot so easily be lost. In common sense, taking appearance for reality, the earth may still be flat and the sun still rise in the east.

Intuition as a source of knowledge assumes the sign is or is always accompanied by the reality. But "Beauty is truth, truth beauty.— that is all ye know on earth, and all ye need to know" (Keats), held true by the Romantics, may be true only in the world of art (on the Grecian urn). The urn (which speaks of death or timeless art) should remind us this is not a morally ideal world where sign and reality are inseparable. Pleasure may not be, and often is not, goodness.

Empiricism which holds that all knowledge is based on sense experience ends in Humean skepticism, or in science based on uncritically held naturalism. But empiricism and its consequential metaphysical naturalism is not self-evident or evident to the senses and cannot be merely imperiously or dogmatically assumed.

The alternative of rationalism has an equally sorry history—where reason is used as a source of truth (Descartes' *Cogito or* Jefferson's *Declaration*) rather than a test for meaning; or used constructively (Plato or Hegel) and not first critically; or used critically, but insufficiently at the basic level (Kant or Nietzsche or Nagarjuna). RP seeks to learn from epistemological history and not repeat deadly errors from the past.

Thinking by nature is presuppositional: we think of the less basic in light of the more basic. In concepts, we think of the finite and temporal in light of the infinite and eternal which are most basic concepts. In judgments that are true or false we think of truth in light of meaning and meaning in light of reason, which, as the laws of thought, is most basic. In argument, we think of conclusion in light of premises. In each case, if we agree on the more basic, we can and will agree on the less basic.

There is diversity *and* unity in all of life, if and only if the order of things is absurd. In philosophy: epistemology, then metaphysics and ethics; in theology: creation, then fall and redemption; In human personality: thought, then feeling and will; aspects recognized in truth, beauty and goodness; in knowledge, holiness and righteousness; in modern western civilization in rationalism, romanticism and realism; in Indian thought: in *jnana, bhakti* and *karma* yoga; and in many other ways. If we observe RP, if we agree on the logically more basic in public discourse we can and will agree on the logically less basic. In a step-by-step process, we can move from foundation to fullness. But in actual human situations we must first address the existentially more basic (the subjective, the ethical, what is good and evil) in order that we can get back to the logically (objectively) more basic.

These three prior factors of common ground lead to the fourth and final, which is the Principle of Clarity (PC). PC states that some things are clear; the basics things are clear; the basic things (in metaphysics, about God and man) in ethics (about good and evil) are clear to reason (epistemology). PC is opposed to skepticism (ancient, modern and postmodern) and to fideism (theistic and non-theistic), that is, belief without proof based on understanding.

Some things *are* clear. If nothing were clear then no logical distinction (between being and non-being, true and false, good and evil) would be clear. No distinction would be meaningful. Thought and discourse would be impossible insofar as we have integrity. Without integrity, we are left in logical and existential absurdity. Therefore, in so far as we think and talk, some things *must* be clear.

The *basic* things are clear. Given RP, if basic things were *not* clear, then nothing would be clear. But some things are clear, from above. Therefore, basic things *are* clear. And the basic things are about metaphysics (God and man), ethics (about good and evil) and epistemology (meaning tested by reason—the laws of thought).

PC, at this point, says only that in principle basic things are clear to reason. It does not settle disputes between the two sets of presuppositions. PC says only that the disputes can and should be settled if we are, with integrity, to think of the talk at all. But in saying this, PC over comes *in principle* both skepticism and fideism. And that, given the history of mankind, is a giant leap for mankind. Thinking is not short circuited, and discourse can begin.

Based on Common Ground, the steps ahead for RP can be identified. One, must there be something eternal? Two, if so, is all or only some eternal? Three, if only some is eternal (God, the creator), is it by special creation? Four, if so, how can the problem of evil be answered in philosophy of religion? Five, only then can the necessity for a special revelation be addressed. Six, if so, which special revelation is consistent with clear general revelation (from one to five above)? Seven, is special revelation continuing or complete? Eight, can PC overcome fideism and settle disputes among theists? And finally, nine, given the problem of evil, can PC settle remaining disputes from skepticism? Can the work of settling disputes be completed based on common ground? The answer of PC, based on Common Ground, is yes.

Without common ground for internal and external disputes, we will strain of gnats and swallow camels. This kind of public discourse leaves a bad taste in the mouth, and intellectual indigestion within. *With* common ground, public discourse is honey, and it is money.

What is Public Philosophy?

Kelly Fitzsimmons Burton, Ph.D.

Increasing political division, the awareness of a crisis in higher education, and the general breakdown of public discourse have caused a growing interest in public philosophy. Some fear that the very foundation of Western Civilization is crumbling. And since Western Civilization is founded upon Western Philosophy, there is a growing suspicion that academic philosophy has been failing in its duty to provide a coherent foundation for the common good. The dominant philosophy in the West today is rarefied, skeptical, and confined to specialists in the field within the halls of the academy. Many people are saying that public philosophy is necessary for the survival of the discipline of philosophy, but it is also essential for the survival of civilization. But what exactly is public philosophy? What is its nature, and why is it necessary?

Public

What is public is what is common. What is common is what is shared by all. So public philosophy is a shared philosophy. But, public also has to do with our life together, the polis, the political. Aristotle said that human beings are rational, political, animals. Public philosophy has to do with the basis for our shared life together or the common good.

Public philosophy addresses those in the public realm who are capable of and desire to argue for foundational truths for the public good. Public philosophy is addressed both to an audience of the public and is for the good of the public. What counts as the public sphere changes with each era. In our age, it may take the form of public lectures, public societies, podcasts, blog posts, journal articles, interaction on social media platforms, conversations in coffee houses, YouTube videos, and much more. Public philosophy is only limited by our imaginations. Any shared space can become an opportunity to do public philosophy.

Philosophy

What is philosophy? Philosophy may be defined by its several features. Philosophy, in its most basic form, is an area of study that deals with foundational questions. These foundational questions include how do I know? What is real? And what is the good life? If we don't answer these foundational questions, we cannot hope to find answers to less foundational questions such as questions of applied ethics and politics.

Philosophy is a way of life that is concerned with the love of wisdom. Wisdom is necessary to live a good life for oneself, but it is also necessary for the common good and knowing how best to structure and order the institutions of culture. Currently, our world could use more wisdom. Wisdom involves knowing the good and the most appropriate means of achieving the good in any and every context of life. Wisdom is cumulative, not arising from a single individual or generation; it is transgenerational and transcultural. We should have the cumulative wisdom of the ages passed on to us through our education. But somehow the cumulative wisdom of the ages has been lost. Can we retrieve the wisdom of the ages? And if so, must we engage in philosophy, the love of wisdom, to do so?

Philosophy is most identifiable by its methodology, the critical use of reason. The critical use of reason necessitates understanding what reason is. Reason is essentially the laws of thought. The laws of thought include the law identity (a is a), the law of non-contradiction (not both a and non-a in the same respect and at the same time), and the law of excluded middle (either a or non-a). The laws of thought are not fallible, but our use of these laws is fallible. This is why we need to be trained in critical thinking.

Our first use of reason is to form concepts, judgments, and arguments, which are the forms of all thought. Concepts grasp the essential nature of a thing and name that thing with a word, term, or other symbol. Concepts are more or less meaningful depending upon our grasp of them. For example, the word "God" expresses a concept. Many disagree on the meaning of the word, so we can take time to define words and clarify meaning until we understand what idea the word communicates. Socrates spent much time pursuing the definitions of words in a desire to understand the reality that words represent.

Judgments are when we put two concepts together with "is" or "is not" in affirmation or negation. For example, "God is good" is a judgment. Judgments are either true or false. Judgments such as "God is good" may be supported by an argument. Arguments are proofs and are either sound or unsound. Knowledge is gained by means of arguments. We can see that there is an order to our thinking from meaning, to truth, to knowledge. In addition to using reason to form concepts, judgments, and arguments, we use reason as a test for meaning. This is the critical use of reason. We use reason to interpret all of our experiences in light of our basic beliefs. Lastly, we use reason to form a coherent world and life view.

We all use reason because it is an aspect of our nature as human beings. We are rational beings. Reason in us is natural. It is not cultural, and it is not conventional. Words are conventional, but concepts are universal. Reason is an aspect of reality; in philosophy, we say reason is ontological. This means that it applies to being, all of being. Being is what exists, what is. Reason grasps being. Reason also puts restrictions on being. Reason tells us that there are no square circles, there are no uncaused events, and there is no being from non-being. Reason is our common source of authority. Because we are all rational beings, we all have recourse to the laws of thought. Anytime words are being used, in any form of authority, be it religious, political, parental, or otherwise, reason is being used and what is said can be tested for meaning. Reason is authoritative for public philosophy. Lastly, reason is fundamental in our human personality. We have thoughts, emotions, and will, and these are ordered from thoughts to emotion to action/will. Reason, when used well, is the source of our greatest good. And when used poorly, or not used at all, it is the source of our deepest misery. This is because we need meaning. Reason is the instrument for obtaining meaning.

Reason provides the tools for doing philosophy. The method of philosophy includes understanding what things mean; meaning is more basic than truth. If we don't understand what something means we cannot know whether it is true or not. Once we have grasped meaning, we can pursue truth. Philosophy is concerned with the truth of the matter. Contemporary philosophy doubts that knowledge of the truth is possible. This is called skepticism, which says nobody can really know for sure. The religious version of this doubt is called fideism, which says nobody can really know for sure but you just have to believe anyway. Both skepticism and fideism deny the possibility of knowledge and, consequently, they deny the possibility of doing philosophy.

Philosophy requires self-examination. It is easy to be outward-looking critiquing other people's views, but philosophy requires that we look inwardly at our own views first. This is consistent with Socrates claim that the unexamined life is not worth living, and with the motto "know thyself." Self-examination is a necessary component to knowing what is true. If we want to know what is true, we have to seek after it. And when we know what is true, then we can show what is true. Knowing involves showing. This is propositional knowledge, not subjective experiential knowledge by acquaintance. Knowledge as objective is fundamental to public philosophy. Knowledge is not the same as holding an opinion or a belief. Opinions and beliefs can be merely subjective and are often mistaken. Knowledge is objective and can be defended publicly by means of reason and argument.

Objective knowledge is shared. What is subjective, relative, and personal, is not relevant for public philosophy. This is because it is not shared by all. And because it is not shared by all, it is not persuasive. Appeal to emotion, or the will to power, is not appropriate for public philosophy either because they bypass our common rationality. These kinds of appeals are essentially dehumanizing. Emotionalism and the will to power are often resorted to when we fail to have reasons for our beliefs.

On the other hand, we may reason well, and provide sound arguments in public discourse, and still fail to persuade our listeners. Failure to persuade may be because our conversation partners are not committed to knowing and pursuing what is true. Public philosophy, in order to be successful, will require a commitment to the pursuit of what is true. What is true is what is according to reality, and not merely to how I feel, or what I want, which are changeable. Truth, as reflecting reality, is not changeable.

Truth is not merely piecemeal, it is systematic. Philosophy helps us to build a coherent world and life view, or a system of philosophy, or our philosophy of life. Our philosophy of life begins with our epistemology, then our metaphysics, and then ethics and all that comes with it. Philosophy helps us to see whether our philosophy of life is coherent and consistent. All people have a world and life view. Not all people have tested their world and life view for meaning. And so some philosophies of life do not provide the meaning we so desperately need. An existential sense of meaninglessness is a sign that one should check one's philosophy of life for coherence at the basic level. The history

13

of ideas is the history of the conflict between different philosophical systems. Not all philosophical systems are equally coherent, and some have become obsolete. When a philosophy ceases to provide meaning, people will cease to defend that philosophy. This is true of Western philosophy as well. Who would defend Western philosophy if it is perceived to be meaningless? In fact, if it is meaningless, it should be abandoned. Some of us are not ready to go that way yet, and thus we must slog through the errors of the history of ideas, sorting the good from the bad.

Human beings are meaning seekers. We need meaning more than anything else. We gain meaning through our view of the good life, which is part of our world and life view. The good for human beings is based on human nature. Human nature is fundamentally rational. The good then, for humans, is the use of reason to the fullest. Reason used to the fullest gives us understanding of the nature of reality. As we understand and pursue a fuller understanding, we find meaning, grow and mature, and find satisfaction and fullness of life. This is what we most desire. And we cannot get it without doing philosophy well.

We are rational, political animals. That we are political means that we live in community with other humans. We are born ignorant and need to be taught about the good life. This means that we are necessarily dependent on the human community and the institutions of culture to know what is good and the means to the good. We cannot do philosophy independently. Philosophy then is necessarily a public work. It requires the human community, and the human community needs to know what the common good is. Human society is a society of rational beings. Participation in human society depends on our exercise of that rationality. We can do it well, or we can do it poorly. If we do it poorly, we will be excluded more and more from the human community.

Human beings as rational beings have a need for philosophy, and human beings as political beings have an obligation to do philosophy. Philosophy done together, in the polis and for the polis, is public philosophy. It is the corporate, cumulative, communal, and cooperative pursuit of what is good for the individual, for the community, and the future.

Public Philosophy

Public Philosophy includes offense and defense. Philosophy on the offense seeks the truth and seeks to know what is good and what is beautiful. It seeks to know the moral law and applications of the moral law to all of life. Philosophy on the defense seeks to critique what is harmful to the true, the good, and the beautiful. It seeks to root out moral evil and its effects on the individual and the community. Defensive philosophy is critical philosophy. It is the critical use of reason to test for meaning, to discard what is meaningless, and defend what is meaningful against all objections.

Public philosophy is not merely activist philosophy. Activist philosophy seeks to rectify social injustices. But social justice requires that we understand the good for society and what is just. These are more fundamental questions. Therefore activist philosophy depends upon foundational philosophy. Foundational philosophy is an offensive philosophy. We must know what is true in order to know what is just. No truth, no justice. Contemporary activist philosophy comes loaded with philosophical assumptions. Defensive philosophy must test those assumptions critically to see whether those assumptions are meaningful, matching reality, and are therefore true. Activist philosophy without defending its presuppositions may turn out to be harmful to society. It is criticism without offering a defensible constructive philosophy. This turns out to be nihilistic self-destruction. Activist philosophy without foundational philosophy becomes dangerously critical of the foundations of the community.

15

Public philosophy must be bold and daring, willing to go where many have not desired to go in the recent past. We must ask and answer questions about metaphysics, what is real. For the past century, we have given up on metaphysics. Once we answer the questions in metaphysics in a positive way that gives us knowledge, we can go on to answer questions about what is good, what is virtuous, and what will make us ultimately happy. Often times answering these questions may feel like "religion." Religion, based upon scripture, is not shared by all people. And because it is not shared, this kind of religion cannot be the basis for public life. But there is something called natural religion. Natural religion is what can be known by all people everywhere at all times about God, and is thus fit for public discourse. Public Philosophy must address the question: is there a God, or is there not a God? If we can't address this question and defend our answer, there is no point in moving ahead. If the answer to this question is not clear, then questions about ethics and the good life will not be clear either. We must address these foundational questions as the basis of a public philosophy.

Addressing these foundational questions is going to press us to back up and work on our reasoning abilities. Public philosophy, as shared discourse, is the shared give-and-take of reasons. We must understand what reason is, and how to use reason well. Therefore, addressing these foundational questions may force us to go back and master basic reasoning skills. We may have to do something like public logic. Public philosophy will require us to begin with the question of how do we know things?

Common Ground for Public Philosophy

Before we can start reasoning with one another in the public sphere, we will have to establish common ground for reasoning with one another. This common ground will require us to take time to understand reason and to commit to the laws of thought when reasoning with one another.

Common ground will require of us that when we commit to a position we live with the implications of that position. This is called integrity. Integrity is consistency between what we say and what we do. If we commit to a position, we should be willing to live with that position and all of its consequences. Furthermore, if we find incoherence in our position, we should be willing to change our position. We should be willing to give up a false assumption rather than giving up on reason. But if we do give up on reason, we should also give up dialogue. Dialogue assumes reason, and we cannot both assume reason and give up reason at the same time and be taken seriously.

Common ground will require that we address more basic issues prior to addressing less basic issues. We are talking about logically more basic issues. If we find answers to more basic questions together, we can find answers to less basic questions together. This is hopeful for making progress in finding meaning and in settling the disputes among human beings. There are many disputes among human beings, and this could be quite daunting. But our hope is that there is a method for addressing disputes. This method is presuppositional thinking, which assumes that we should address more basic questions prior to addressing less basic questions. For instance, meaning is logically more basic than truth. We must understand what a statement means before we can say whether that statement is true or not. Another example is that premises in an argument are logically prior to the conclusion to an argument. If we can agree on the more basic we can agree on the less basic and this is hopeful.

Lastly, common ground will require that we are committed to the principle of clarity. The principle of clarity states that some things are clear. Clear means they are easily knowable. Easily knowable means that all humans who want to know can know, and that all human beings who can know ought to know. There's a moral obligation to knowing what is clear. What is clear to reason? Basic philosophical assumptions about God and man and good and evil are clear to reason. For instance, it is clear that either God exists or God does not exist. It is clear what is the good and what is not the good. It is clear that we know by reason or we don't know by reason. If we cannot agree to common ground, then we cannot engage in public discourse.

The main obstacles to common ground are skepticism and fideism, both of which deny that some things are clear to reason. Therefore skeptics and fideists will not readily engage in public philosophy and may seek to hinder it. The question is, are skeptics and fideists willing to have integrity and live with the implications of their position? If nobody can really know, then why engage in public discourse? If we aren't dialoguing to find knowledge, then what are we doing? If knowledge is not possible, we should just be silent and go home.

Virtues of Public Philosophy

Public philosophy, as pursuit of the common good, will require certain virtues. Knowing the good involves doing the good. Knowing the common good requires doing the common good. Doing involves virtue. If we know the goal, we will know the most appropriate virtues for achieving that goal. Public philosophy involves public discourse. Public discourse will require that we have wisdom in how we communicate with our fellow human beings. This requires interpersonal skills. Public philosophy will require that we love the good, and we love our fellow human beings. Another virtue necessary for doing public philosophy is hope that the good can and will be achieved. It requires a rugged, dogged, gradual idealism.

Those who do public philosophy will have to be patient, persevering, and gritty. There will be much opposition, so those engaging in public philosophy will need courage. They will need to be willing and able to say hard things in the face of public opposition. Progress in knowing and pursuing what is true in the public realm is going to take a lot of hard work. It's going to require friendship. Friendship is the effect of mutual commitment to the good. The work of friends will require coordination, cooperation, and the unity of the diversity of gifts and abilities for the pursuit of the good life for ourselves and for the polis. The community of friends will need to rebuild the broken institutions of culture. Knowing the nature of these institutions is part of public philosophy.

Once we have answered the question of what is the good, and the common good, we can go on and address questions of the polis. What is the nature and purpose of the family? What is the nature and purpose of the church? What is the nature and purpose of the government? What is the nature and purpose of education? What is the nature and purpose of the economy and business? These are the basic institutions of culture. While we're at it, we should ask the question what is culture? What is civilization? What is the basis of a lasting civilization? These are exciting questions, and we should be addressing them publicly. So come, let's reason together. Let's find answers and let the rebuilding commence.

Conclusion

To sum up: Philosophy is an area of study that is not merely relegated to the academy, it is an attitude which includes the love of wisdom; it is a method which includes the critical use of reason; it is an application to ourselves in self-examination; it is systematic and involves constructing a coherent philosophy of life that is based on what is real and true. A philosophy of life based on what is true will determine what is good for ourselves and for the community. Public philosophy is philosophy done with the goal of good life for the human community.

Why Study the Humanities?

Owen Anderson, Ph.D.

The general topic of this paper is "why study the humanities?" I will address this topic as it relates to several literary works. For me, this topic arose in couple of ways. I have been especially studying this question about the humanities this year. I am the Faculty Senate president for Arizona State University West, and as part of that office, my duty is to complete a research assignment. Mine was to look at ways that humanities graduate students find employment outside of teaching. This is a very practical question and can be studied by following the progress of students after graduation. But it raises the larger question about why study the humanities? It is only related to the practical question of what job we will do with a humanities degree? What I am going to argue for here is that the study of the humanities is to find meaning, and we find meaning by using reason to understand the nature of things. That means as we approach the humanities, we are assuming that we can know, and this assumes that some things are clear. This will become clearer as we continue.

But I have been interested in this question for a long time. I attended Wickenburg high school and was introduced to the great books. We read some wonderful literature, and I still remember our discussions. I was introduced to art, and art displays for us the individual and through that takes us to the universal. What this did was introduced me to the human questions that I wanted to answer. Although my education raised these questions, I noticed they weren't being

21

answered. I noticed that many people asked these questions and felt confident in their answers but didn't actually have knowledge. I didn't want just a belief or even a true belief, I wanted to know. And so, this started me on the road of studying these questions in the academy. I have always held the humanities in high esteem and was eager to think about the benefits of studying them.

It is common to find posters in philosophy departments about the kinds of jobs a person can get with a philosophy degree. It has also made news that some colleges are cutting humanities majors (the University of Wisconsin at Stevens Point). This led me to a Stanley Fish article in the Chronicle of Higher Education titled "Stop Trying to Sell the Humanities: Arguments that they're useful are wrong, anti-humanistic, and sure to backfire" (June 17, 2018). Here he considers some of the most common arguments to motivate students to pursue a humanities degree: it will help you get a better job; it makes you a better citizen; it makes you a better person. The idea that it will help you get a better job can be analyzed empirically and reduces the humanities to a means to some other end like money or comfort. The claim that it makes a better citizen or somehow is necessary for democracy is contrary to the idea that humans have access to common sense, or what they need to know for a virtuous life, and instead suggests that elites in the academy are best able to tell the population how to live. And to the idea that this study makes you a better person, Fish says that whoever makes this claim has not spent much time around Philosophy and English faculty.

So why study the humanities? Really, we can ask the broader question of why study? We study to know things. What kinds of things do we want to know, and why do we want to know them? We make distinctions between the kinds of things we want to know, perhaps saying some are more relevant to our ends and some less relevant. But this requires that we have known the end we ought to pursue. We can also make a distinction between basic and less basic. A belief is less basic or not basic when it has presuppositions. We can work our way back to our most basic beliefs. We do this in all of the disciplines we study. We begin with numbers, not calculus. We start with the ABC's, not Tolstoy.

We have already mentioned an example. We want to know what is good. This gives us two basic questions. How do we know? And what is good? These are linked to the question "what is real?" because what is good for a thing is based on the nature of a thing. We want to know what is real, what is, and from there to what is good. We want to know what is real so we can pursue what is good.

And the humanities study these three basic questions. We distinguish the humanities and the natural sciences. Where the natural sciences study the laws governing the material world, the humanities study the human condition in all of its expressions. Attempts to reduce one of these to the other, say to reduce humans to a material object or reduce the material world to an idea, fail as the reality of each resists and prevents this reductionism.

The humanities are a study of human nature and the human condition. There is an element in these studies that we do not find in the natural sciences. We find the moral element, the reality of choice and human nature, that is not found in the study of the natural world. And this is what we will be looking at here in our reading selections. What does it mean to be a human? What is the human condition? Specifically, why do we suffer, and can we make any sense of our suffering? Is there meaning in life?

Something happens when we begin asking these questions. We quickly begin to see our need for meaning, for understanding. Meaning can mean purpose, and we see it studied this way in the natural sciences. But here it also means understanding or cognitive content. We are pursuing meaning when we ask what something is. And this illuminates its relationship to reason. Reason, as the laws of thought, is that by which we understand. We make distinctions to understand. We distinguish between a and non-a. Or human and non-human. Or good and non-good. Or God and non-God. When we contradict ourselves, saying that a is non-a, or human is non-human, or God is non-God, we lose meaning.

These are connected: our use of reason and finding meaning or understanding. When we study the humanities, we are using reason to study humans, including their lack of consistency in using reason and the consequences of this. We will consider attempts to get around this in the concrete examples of our texts. But these come in only a few forms of anti-reason. These are non-cognitive in the sense that they attempt to bypass beliefs in their attempt to avoid reason. Instead, they might emphasize the practical (as we will see with Ivan Ilych) and live in an uncritical manner assuming what works. Or they might be mystical in emphasizing an experiential acquaintance or awareness. In either case, these cannot be articulated or explained without stepping into the cognitive, forming beliefs about what works or what is the object of this mystical experience, and thus using reason to try and find meaning.

We might think that the avoidance of reason could go on forever in a given person's life. And indeed, it might. There is no reason to think that someone who denies reason will ever begin to use it of their own accord. Just the opposite. If someone is denying reason, then they cannot reason their way to seeing why they need reason. They may be in the continual self-referentially absurd state of giving reasons to justify their doubt and denial of reason. This is the awful inconsistency of the human condition that is a kind of death.

Death is when something is no longer functioning. We usually just think of this in terms of physical death. Our body stops functioning. It still exists. In fact, we have to dispose of dead bodies properly. But we can see that there is also another kind of death. Our mind can stop functioning. It still exists. But it hasn't found meaning or understanding. This condition of meaninglessness is abhorrent, and people do all kinds of things (short of actually using reason to start thinking) to dull and numb this. What is meaningless is boring. Meaninglessness and boredom come together. And the tension between our ability to use reason and our own failure to so do without anyone else to blame brings guilt. These three constitute spiritual death: meaninglessness, boredom, and guilt.

Notice how meaninglessness is the consequence of not using reason. It is when we fail to make basic distinctions, or even deny that there are basic distinctions. It is the denial that anything is clear. By way of contrast, when we see what is clear, we understand and having meaning. This is why understanding is described as light, and ignorance, meaningless, boredom, as darkness. Ivan's turning point is described as light. We might even say we have a fear of there being nothing clear because we see that this results in the denial of all meaning, it results in nihilism. If we cannot know, we cannot understand, then this includes we cannot know what is meaningful.

The reality of spiritual death is a central part of the study of the humanities. And it is a condition that the person denying reason cannot get themselves out of. But it is a condition, the human condition, that raises the problem of redemption. How will we go from denying reason and spiritual death to using reason and a life full of meaning? It isn't through self-help, and it isn't merely a matter of needing a coach to show us the way. The guilt involved shows that there is a need for redemption, we were given something that we wasted, and now we are in debt. How will we be brought out of this condition and the debt be paid? Sometimes this is called atonement, and we will see how it appears in the Gerard Manly Hopkins poems and in Ivan Ilych's death (but we really see it in his life). Because we are guilty, and we cannot earn redemption, there is a need for grace.

This brings us back to a previous question: What will get us to stop and think in the condition of not thinking? In the poems and the short story that we will look at, we will see that natural evil is what gets us to stop and think. Natural evil, all forms of suffering, is a call back from moral evil. In the condition of moral evil and its consequence of spiritual death, we would never stop and think. Natural evil is imposed on us, it interrupts our life, as a call back to stop and think.

If we had no moral evil, we would have no natural evil. Which means, if we have natural evil, we have moral evil. It is this realization that Ivan resists so strongly. It is this process that Hopkins describes in his poem "Carrion Comfort."

Before we turn to these texts to illustrate these points, let me again address the question of the humanities. Why study? Why think? Why try to understand? The alternative is not to think. This could be the simple life, the simpleton. It might just be that a person wanted to pursue a pleasant life and hadn't given it much thought. The simpleton says that knowledge is not needed. The simpleton doesn't know and doesn't care to know. Or we could consider the fool. The fool believes he knows. The fool is blinded by pride. There is ontological pride where we put ourselves in the place of God. And this produces epistemological pride where we think we know and don't need to seek (God knows all things and doesn't need to seek). We will see examples of both in Tolstoy. Neither the simpleton nor the fool has any need for the humanities. Their life is like chaff, it is barren, it has no fruit. The alternative is what is exemplified in the Socratic dictum: the unexamined life is not worth living, or, is less than human existence. To aim at excellence is to aim at understanding. In art, we study the individual and what it expresses about the universal.

This is how the distinction mentioned earlier between the humanities and the natural sciences is united. As humans, we use reason to understand the nature of things. This includes the nature of things in the material world. We will be considering examples of this in Hopkins' "As Kingfishers Catch Fire." And the nature of things created reveals the nature of the Creator. The glory revealed in the natural world, the excellence, is a revelation of the glory, the excellence, of the Creator. And so, we have united here the role of Creator and Redeemer, and Hopkins uses a specific word for this.

If the humanities, or someone claiming to teach us the humanities, cannot teach us these things, then they are not worth studying. Or, since the humanities do reveal these things, it is the supposed teacher of the humanities who cannot show what is clear that must be exposed. What is important is not the finding of a place to get a diploma so that you can get a job. That is a different discussion and important in its own way. What is important for studying the humanities is to find one who knows what is clear about these basic questions and can teach you. The student cannot rise above the teacher. This is true if the teacher is a simpleton, a fool, or has wisdom.

And that last term is one we associate with understanding what is good, with the fulfillment of the humanities. The fool and the simpleton will not recognize the wise. Indeed, one of the easiest ways to identify a fool is that he scoffs at, mocks, the wise. Those who put themselves in place to teach without themselves knowing the basics must go back and learn the first things. There are few things more harmful than someone who puts themselves in a place to teach without knowledge. Avoid such as these while seeking out the wise teacher and then learn all you can from that person. Test those who claim to be teachers, ask them if they know or only think they know.

Gerard Manly Hopkins

Life will test us. And we are going to look at this in Tolstoy's description. Is it the death of Ivan Ilych or the life of Ivan Ilych? But first, let's look at the Hopkins poems. What I want to do here for each reading is not look at some key ideas that will then help us both with the question why study the humanities and also aid our deeper discussion later today. I want to consider poems in this order:

Spring and Fall
to a young child

27

Márgarét, áre you gríeving
Over Goldengrove unleaving?
Leáves like the things of man, you
With your fresh thoughts care for, can you?
Ah! ás the heart grows older
It will come to such sights colder
By and by, nor spare a sigh
Though worlds of wanwood leafmeal lie;
And yet you wíll weep and know why.
Now no matter, child, the name:
Sórrow's spríngs áre the same.
Nor mouth had, no nor mind, expressed
What heart heard of, ghost guessed:
It ís the blight man was born for,
It is Margaret you mourn for.

Think about how these themes illustrate what we discussed above. The title itself. Spring and Fall (not autumn, the British usage). The human condition involves a fall. It involves both moral evil and natural evil. We yearn for the spring, the restoration of life, both the original before evil and the restoration from redemption. Here we find this yearning in a child as leaves die. But this ultimately points us to her own death. And we mourn over death. It is "natural" evil, but it is not natural. We were not created to die. Natural evil is imposed on a world with moral evil. And natural evil makes us ask why. The question is, will we press through to meaning and answering that question or settle for something less. The next poem makes this more personal:

Carrion Comfort

Not, I'll not, carrion comfort, Despair, not feast on thee;

Not untwist — slack they may be — these last strands of man
In me ór, most weary, cry I can no more. I can;
Can something, hope, wish day come, not choose not to be.
But ah, but O thou terrible, why wouldst thou rude on me
Thy wring-world right foot rock? lay a lionlimb against me? scan
With darksome devouring eyes my bruisèd bones? and fan,
O in turns of tempest, me heaped there; me frantic to avoid thee and
flee?

Why? That my chaff might fly; my grain lie, sheer and clear.
Nay in all that toil, that coil, since (seems) I kissed the rod,
Hand rather, my heart lo! lapped strength, stole joy, would laugh,
chéer.
Cheer whom though? the hero whose heaven-handling flung me, fóot
tród
Me? or me that fought him? O which one? is it each one? That night,
that year
Of now done darkness I wretch lay wrestling with (my God!) my God.

Why not despair? He calls it a carrion comfort. It is animal, it is
less than human, it indulges the flesh. To be human means to reject
despair even as we cannot seem to understand. To despair is to reject
understanding or say understanding is not possible. But we cannot
be human and do that. It is less than human. This meaninglessness is
chaff, worthless, fruitless. And this condition is not merely a matter of
circumstances, it is from God. Why has God done this, lay a lion limb
against us? The concern is to find meaning, it is "why," not merely to
solve the problem and get out of suffering. Why would God permit
this? A solution must reconcile the sovereignty of God with the reality
of natural and moral evil. The author kisses the rod of discipline and
the hand who holds it. In this, he not only avoids despair but finds joy
itself. This is a wrestling with God.

In the next poem, we find an elaboration of this meaning and joy.

We see Hopkins in his description of the individual. The nature of a thing. The nature of a thing, being what it is, displays glory. He gives visual examples and audial examples. He then moves to the human, to the self, living according to its nature, the natural being acts without a kind of thought, but the human introduces the moral dimension and displays the glory of God as the image of God. He speaks here of Christ displayed in human nature, and this use of the term Christ (anointed one) as opposed to Jesus (savior of his people) or Messiah (Hebrew, for anointed one) reminds us of the way Christ is introduced as the logos, the Word of God, that which makes God known. This word of God as the light of man is reason, and this word of God, this logos, is found in the creation although the creation has known it not. The Word of God makes the Father known through human nature.

As Kingfishers Catch Fire

As kingfishers catch fire, dragonflies draw flame;
As tumbled over rim in roundy wells
Stones ring; like each tucked string tells, each hung bell's
Bow swung finds tongue to fling out broad its name;
Each mortal thing does one thing and the same:
Deals out that being indoors each one dwells;
Selves — goes itself; myself it speaks and spells,
Crying Whát I dó is me: for that I came.

I say móre: the just man justices;
Keeps grace: thát keeps all his goings graces;
Acts in God's eye what in God's eye he is —
Chríst — for Christ plays in ten thousand places,
Lovely in limbs, and lovely in eyes not his
To the Father through the features of men's faces.

And finally, the poem dedicated to Christ our Lord. The anointed one, or ruler. The Windhover rules in expressing itself, its nature. He is master of all and seems to effortlessly take his dominion. This points Hopkins to his chevalier, the slow, deliberate ploughing that breaks the soil also displays its excellence, the fall, gall, gash gold vermillion. Christ rules in this, effortlessly like the Windhover, as the Word of God making God known.

The Windhover
To Christ our Lord
I caught this morning morning's minion, king-
dom of daylight's dauphin, dapple-dawn-drawn Falcon, in his riding
Of the rolling level underneath him steady air, and striding
High there, how he rung upon the rein of a wimpling wing
In his ecstasy! then off, off forth on swing,
As a skate's heel sweeps smooth on a bow-bend: the hurl and gliding
Rebuffed the big wind. My heart in hiding
Stirred for a bird, – the achieve of, the mastery of the thing!

Brute beauty and valour and act, oh, air, pride, plume, here
Buckle! AND the fire that breaks from thee then, a billion
Times told lovelier, more dangerous, O my chevalier!

No wonder of it: shéer plód makes plough down sillion shine.

Hopkins moves from the reality of the human condition under natural evil to the personal and excruciating wrestling with this and the joy in coming to understand, to seeing the glory that is revealed in the nature of things and what this reveals about God the Creator and Redeemer. Now, these are also what we find in the life and death of Ivan Ilych. Let's look at some examples. I am assuming familiarity with this story, and so my comments will be somewhat of an outline.

31

The Death of Ivan Ilych

The story begins with a chapter after the death of Ivan. We see how his family, friends, and co-workers process his death and attending a funeral. It is an obligation, a nuisance to some, and mostly brings out self-centered concerns. Playing cards, how hard Ivan's illness was for his wife. Peter, no one, accepts the human condition. Death is treated as a misfortune to others and a hindrance to our own life but not something that will happen to you.

> 'Three days of frightful suffering and then death! Why, that might suddenly, at any time, happen to me,' he thought, and for a moment felt terrified. But — he did not himself know how — the customary reflection at once occurred to him that this had happened to Ivan Ilych and not to him, and that it should not and could not happen to him, and that to think that it could would be yielding to depression which he ought not to do, as Schwartz's expression plainly showed.

Except for Gerasim, who says: "It's God will. We shall all come to it some day," said Gerasim.

In chapter 2, we turn to the chronology of Ivan's life. He begins with all the hopes of youth. He quickly becomes vain. He is pragmatic and sensual. He finds "meaning" in pleasures and seeks a life of pleasure and a job and family that will give him this pleasure. We see that "All the enthusiasms of childhood and youth passed without leaving much trace on him; he succumbed to sensuality, to vanity, and latterly among the highest classes to liberalism, but always within limits which his instinct unfailingly indicated to him as correct."

He accommodates to immorality in order to preserve his pleasant life:

> *At school he had done things which had formerly seemed to him*
> *very horrid and made him feel disgusted with himself when he did*
> *them; but when later on he saw that such actions were done by*
> *people of good position and that they did not regard them as wrong,*
> *he was able not exactly to regard them as right, but to forget about*
> *them entirely or not be at all troubled at remembering them.*

Natural evil as suffering first imposed itself on his life in the form of
marital strife. It is interesting that it is in this area of life that he first
is conscious of natural evil. Marriage was supposed to be pleasant
and add to the pleasures of life. He married almost out of social duty
because that is what you do at this age. But he notices suffering when
it interrupts his pursuit of what he thinks is good. That is when he
responds. Natural evil was all around him, and he had not noticed. Nor
does this natural evil make him consider his own moral evil. Instead,
he stops and thinks only to the consideration of how to minimize the
impact of the strife on his pursuit of pleasure.

Natural evil will make us more consistent: we will either be more
consistent in our denial of reason or our use of reason. Natural
evil presses our self-deception about ourselves and our condition.
We see Ivan's self-deception come out more and more as well as
the self-deception of those around him. This pressing requires self-
justification to defend the self-deception. Natural evil breaks through
these. A person cannot remain unmoved. They will either go deeper
into darkness or repent and begin to use reason to shed self-deception.
We see that "Very soon, within a year of his wedding, Ivan Ilych had
realized that marriage, though it may add some comforts to life, is
in fact a very intricate and difficult affair towards which in order to
perform one's duty, that is, to lead a decorous life approved of by
society, one must adopt a definite attitude just as towards one's official
duties."

His next encounter with natural evil is in his professional life. And this is what he had turned to in order to avoid the strife with his wife. So here, in his solution, he also encounters suffering. Others have let him down. His job has let him down. He cannot get enough money to satisfy his desires. He cannot indulge himself as he wants at this salary. The solution is more money (as opposed to learning what is truly good):

> *This was in 1880, the hardest year of Ivan Ilych's life. It was then that it became evident on the one hand that his salary was insufficient for them to live on, and on the other that he had been forgotten, and not only this, but that what was for him the greatest and most cruel injustice appeared to others a quite ordinary occurrence. Even his father did not consider it his duty to help him. Ivan Ilych felt himself abandoned by everyone, and that they regarded his position with a salary of 3,500 rubles as quite normal and even fortunate. He alone knew that with the consciousness of the injustices done him, with his wife's incessant nagging, and with the debts he had contracted by living beyond his means, his position was far from normal.*

In order to save money that summer, he obtained leave of absence and went with his wife to live in the country at her brother's place. He is first aware of meaninglessness. It is interesting that the term used is "ennui," which especially has to do with dissatisfaction due to lack of excitement. He still is not connecting up his suffering with his failure to know what is good and the spiritual death of meaninglessness. We read: "In the country, without his work, he experienced ennui for the first time in his life, and not only ennui but intolerable depression, and he decided that it was impossible to go on living like that, and that it was necessary to take energetic measures."

He hasn't heeded these early calls back. He has had plenty. Now is the life-altering event: "Once when mounting a step-ladder to show the upholsterer, who did not understand, how he wanted the hangings draped, he made a false step and slipped, but being a strong and agile man he clung on and only knocked his side against the knob of the window frame." His suffering begins slowly. He has time to reflect. His only concern is whether to ignore it because it will get better or to seek medical help. He has a desire to get past natural evil as quickly as possible and get on with the pleasant life. He is not yet hearing suffering as a callback. He does no introspection. He notices that others treat him, as a patient, just like he treated clients in law. His suffering does not matter personally to them, and they enjoy their position of power:

> *All this was just what Ivan Ilych had himself brilliantly accomplished a thousand times in dealing with men on trial. The doctor summed up just as brilliantly, looking over his spectacles triumphantly and even gaily at the accused. From the doctor's summing up Ivan Ilych concluded that things were bad, but that for the doctor, and perhaps for everybody else, it was a matter of indifference, though for him it was bad.*

This is also the first mention of popular religion in his life. Popular religion sets aside the concern for truth and instead focuses on psychological and practical needs. Ivan has viewed himself as above that kind of religion but finds himself listening to the story of a miraculous healing: "One day a lady acquaintance mentioned a cure effected by a wonder-working icon. Ivan Ilych caught himself listening attentively and beginning to believe that it had occurred. This incident alarmed him. "Has my mind really weakened to such an extent?" he asked himself. "Nonsense! It's all rubbish.""

As the suffering increases, he begins to think. He can no longer keep his thoughts on simply getting past natural evil. He wonders about his own mortality, and he can barely fathom that he is mortal. What about this old syllogism (we usually use "Socrates"): "The syllogism he had learnt from Kiesewetter's Logic:

> Caius is a man, men are mortal, therefore Caius is mortal," had
> always seemed to him correct as applied to Caius, but certainly
> not as applied to himself. That Caius — man in the abstract —
> was mortal, was perfectly correct, but he was not Caius, not an
> abstract man, but a creature quite, quite separate from all others.
> He had been little Vanya, with a mamma and a papa, with Mitya
> and Volodya, with the toys, a coachman and a nurse, afterwards
> with Katenka and will all the joys, griefs, and delights of childhood,
> boyhood, and youth. What did Caius know of the smell of that
> striped leather ball Vanya had been so fond of? Had Caius kissed
> his mother's hand like that, and did the silk of her dress rustle
> so for Caius? Had he rioted like that at school when the pastry
> was bad? Had Caius been in love like that? Could Caius preside
> at a session as he did? Caius really was mortal, and it was right
> for him to die; but for me, little Vanya, Ivan Ilych, with all my
> thoughts and emotions, it's altogether a different matter. It cannot
> be that I ought to die. That would be too terrible.

He is in this suffering alone. Others only think of it as it affects them.
They cannot pity him. Not in the selfish way he wants and not in a
real way that would show actual concern. The kind of pity he wants
is another kind of pleasure that he seeks. He has not yet let go of his
view of the good. We see that "Apart from this lying, or because of
it, what most tormented Ivan Ilych was that no one pitied him as he
wished to be pitied."

   As he wrestles with his own mortality, he becomes aware that others
are in the same position he was of not accepting the reality of death.
It is a lie. They do not want to hear the call back any more than he did.
For them to understand it as real would mean that they must deal with
natural evil as a callback and they will not do that. So, they engage in
self-deception. This is why suffering in Ivan's life has been piercing.

36

His self-deception is no longer sufficient. But others are engaged in their own self-deception. And to do this together requires accepting a lie together. When the self-deception is questioned, they engage in self-justification. We see this with his wife throughout and especially in her discussion with Peter at the beginning of the story. Her concern is her own comfort. She has not heard the callback. There is a lie they all agree to accept:

> *What tormented Ivan Ilych most was the deception, the lie, which for some reason they all accepted, that he was not dying but was simply ill, and they only need keep quiet and undergo a treatment, and then something very good would result. He however knew that do what they would nothing would come of it, only still more agonizing suffering and death. This deception tortured him —their not wishing to admit what they all knew and what he knew, but wanting to lie to him concerning his terrible condition, and wishing and forcing him to participate in that lie.*

Finally, he begins to ask basic questions about his life. Natural evil has cut through his self-deception, and he must look at himself and ask what do you want?:

> *'What do I want? To live and not to suffer," he answered.*
> *"Why, to live as I used to — well and pleasantly."*
> *"As you lived before, well and pleasantly?" the voice repeated.*
> *And in imagination he began to recall the best moments of his pleasant life. But strange to say none of those best moments of his pleasant life now seemed at all what they had then seemed — none of them except the first recollections of childhood. There, in childhood, there had been something really pleasant with which it would be possible to live if it could return. But the child who had experienced that happiness existed no longer, it was like a reminiscence of somebody else.*

He comes to see that the pleasant life he had been pursuing is a fantasy of his own making. It is not real. He does not have knowledge. He cannot defend his own beliefs, and they have left him. He moves from looking at himself, asking about his beliefs, to critically analyze them. Perhaps he has been wrong all this time. This is awful to consider by why is it? This is just what he should be considering. Look how much natural evil it has taken for him to get here. He could have done this at the very beginning when he was tempted to vanity and then moral compromise. He could have done this when strife with his wife first emerged. He could have done this when his professional life was not satisfying when he did not have enough money when he experienced ennui. Look how much it has taken to get an otherwise capable individual to finally ask if he has lived the wrong way!

> *"Then what does it mean? Why? It can't be that life is so senseless and horrible. But if it really has been so horrible and senseless, why must I die and die in agony? There is something wrong!*
>
> *"Maybe I did not live as I ought to have done," it suddenly occurred to him. "But how could that be, when I did everything properly? "*

And he is confronted now with the greatest pain. The physical pain is what has occupied all of his attention. Now he finally focuses on spiritual death. The greatest pain is that perhaps there is no answer, no purpose, no meaning. All this horror is meaningless. That is too awful ever to consider. It is hell. He asks himself:

> *"Then what do you want now? To live? Live how? Live as you lived in the law courts when the usher proclaimed 'The judge is coming!' The judge is coming, the judge!" he repeated to himself. "Here he is, the judge. But I am not guilty!" he exclaimed angrily. "What is it for?" And he ceased crying, but turning his face to the wall continued to ponder on the same question: Why, and for what*

*purpose, is there all this horror? But however much he pondered
he found no answer. And whenever the thought occurred to him,
as it often did, that it all resulted from his not having lived as he
ought to have done, he at once recalled the correctness of his whole
life and dismissed so strange an idea.*

Notice how he connects this meaninglessness with "no reason,"
no reason in the sense of no purpose but also of no sense, no
understanding, no meaning. And no reason means there is nothing,
nihilism. When we deny reason, we end in nihilism. And it has taken
natural evil to get this into focus for Ivan: "'Why these sufferings?'
And the voice answered, 'For no reason — they just are so.' Beyond
and besides this there was nothing.'"

Now he begins to connect the increasing intensity of natural evil
with his own increasing spiritual death. The physical death increases
only as a call back from his spiritual death. There are two senses of
Ivan's death. He has been dead this whole time. The death of Ivan Ilych
is not at the end. He has been dead, and this approaching physical
death calls him to think about this condition, and we see him start to
do this: "'Just as the pain went on getting worse and worse, so my life
grew worse and worse,' he thought. 'There is one bright spot there at
the back, at the beginning of life, and afterwards all becomes blacker
and blacker and proceeds more and more rapidly — in inverse ratio
to the square of the distance from death,' thought Ivan Ilych.'"

The only explanation, the only solution, is understanding. It is to
make sense of the suffering. To have meaning. The only solution in
that direction is that Ivan has not lived as he ought to have lived.
But that requires repentance of an entire life of false beliefs, self-
deception, and self-justification. He would have to take responsibility
for having done this. There is no one else to blame: "There is one
possible explanation: "Resistance is impossible!" he said to himself. "If
I could only understand what it is all for! But that too is impossible. An
explanation would be possible if it could be said that I have not lived as

I ought to. But it is impossible to say that." Again, his suffering is not primarily the physical, it is now the spiritual, the lack of meaning and the realization that he has been wrong: "His mental sufferings were due to the fact that that night, as he looked at Gerasim's sleepy, good-natured face with its prominent cheek-bones, the question suddenly occurred to him: "What if my whole life has been wrong?' "

It is finally when he can accept that he has not lived as he should have that he begins to make sense of his life. He can no longer defend himself. He sees self-justification for what it is. A continuation of the lie. His belief about the good as pleasure has been false. What a realization! And what did it take to get there? Are we any different? What do you expect out of life? Will you live an easy and pleasant life, or will you need to suffer? Notice also that he comes to a point where he says he has no defense. This is part of his past legal training. He cannot defend how he has lived. He has no excuse. He is culpable. Guilty. His life had been chaff:

> It occurred to him that what had appeared perfectly impossible before, namely that he had not spent his life as he should have done, might after all be true. It occurred to him that his scarcely perceptible attempts to struggle against what was considered good by the most highly placed people, those scarcely noticeable impulses which he had immediately suppressed, might have been the real thing, and all the rest false. And his professional duties and the whole arrangement of his life and of his family, and all his social and official interests, might all have been false. He tried to defend all those things to himself and suddenly felt the weakness of what he was defending. There was nothing to defend.

In general, his pragmatic, pleasant life had not required popular religion. Popular religion seeks to keep our self-deception and self-justification in place while giving psychological comfort. Early, when he heard about miracles, he rebuked himself for listening. Now he engaged in this ritual, it provides initial psychological relief, but this is not lasting. It is non-cogitative. It is an uninterpreted experience, and so has no meaning. And that is what has been the problem all along, lack of meaning. Adding more meaninglessness will not be the solution.

Popular religion only masks the doubts but does not answer them: "When the priest came and heard his confession, Ivan Ilych was softened and seemed to feel a relief from his doubts and consequently from his sufferings, and for a moment there came a ray of hope. He again began to think of the vermiform appendix and the possibility of correcting it. He received the sacrament with tears in his eyes. When they laid him down again afterwards he felt a moment's ease, and the hope that he might live awoke in him again. He began to think of the operation that had been suggested to him. "To live! I want to live!" he said to himself."

His realization about his entire life grows as the physical pain grows:

> Her dress, her figure, the expression of her face, the tone of her voice, all revealed the same thing. "This is wrong, it is not as it should be. All you have lived for and still live for is falsehood and deception, hiding life and death from you." And as soon as he admitted that thought, his hatred and his agonizing physical suffering again sprang up, and with that suffering a consciousness of the unavoidable, approaching end. And to this was added a new sensation of grinding shooting pain and a feeling of suffocation.

Now we see the use of the term "light." This is a typical image for understanding. Not only has his life not been what it should have been, this is his own fault, and he can repent. He now can start thinking about what the right thing is. And look what it took to get here. Are we any different? We see: "At that very moment Ivan Ilych fell through and caught sight of the light, and it was revealed to him that though his life had not been what it should have been, this could still be rectified.

He asked himself, "What is the right thing?" and grew still, listening."

Notice the timing, the drama here, as he dies, he also comes to life. His last spoken word is to repent, to ask forgiveness. Who is he asking? The one who matters, and it is that one who will understand. We might want Tolstoy to go into this more, to tell us more about what Ivan experiences as he dies, the "other side." But that is part of the very problem Ivan has needed to overcome, and Tolstoy does not indulge us. He gives us what we need, it is what Ivan needed. It is the most important part of this whole story. The death of Ivan Ilych was the source of his life. Or, Ivan has been dead from the beginning, but physical death was a call back to stop and consider his spiritual death. In place of spiritual death, there is now light. He understands. Spiritual death is finished, it is no more. The image of light cannot refer to physical death as he then dies. But the power of physical death is gone as well. It has served its purpose. He is now alive.

> He tried to add, "Forgive me," but said "Forego" and waved his hand, knowing that He whose understanding mattered would understand." Again: "He sought his former accustomed fear of death and did not find it. "Where is it? What death?" There was no fear because there was no death." In place of death there was light: "'Death is finished," he said to himself. "It is no more!"

Notice the role of God here. He is present in the entire story and never directly mentioned. Only referenced at the end as the one to whom we present and who understands our asking forgiveness. This means that God is the one who provides redemption. And God is the one who has used natural evil to get Ivan to stop and think. God has not been silent, hidden, distant, aloof, for Ivan. God has been there from the beginning of the story actively involved in Ivan's life, and it took all of this for Ivan to see this at his last moment finally. Will we see it sooner? Are we different?

Conclusion and summary: The works of art we have considered

have laid bare to us the human condition. This is primarily expressed in the reality of suffering and our need to make sense of it. It is found in the excellence displayed in the nature of things and how we have not understood what is clear. The study of the humanities brings us to the human condition and to the nature of things. We begin at the beginning with basic questions: how do we know? What is real? What is good? If the humanities cannot answer these, if the humanities teach that nothing is clear, then they are of no value; they are meaningless. But if the humanities affirm that some things are clear to reason and that among these are the good and the meaning in suffering, then they are the source of our greatest joy. The study of the nature of things reveals the nature of their Creator. The human condition includes both natural evil and moral evil. It is the fear of the consequences of moral evil, meaninglessness, that is the beginning of this study, the beginning of wisdom. We can test those who sit in the chair of the humanities teacher to see if they are wise or only think they are wise if they know or only think they know. We study the humanities because we love wisdom, and we want to know what is good. When you are considering where to study, you will need to find someone who knows and can teach you these things.

Religion and Science: Breaking the Spell

Rodney Tussing, Ph.D.

This paper was first delivered in February, 2019, as a lecture for Paradise Valley Community College's Public Philosophy lecture series. My thesis for this paper and for my book, is that the two-category approach to the world's belief systems, commonly understood as religion and science, is inadequate and needs to be deconstructed and reformulated.[2] It's time for a 'paradigm shift.' You might be wondering at the start, so, how does a work on Religion and Science fit into this public philosophy journal? Here's how. Both categories of what we refer to as Religion and science are constructed upon foundational beliefs that are essentially philosophical. That is, they each make judgments about the nature of the world, the universe, human life—about existence, about what ultimately exists. These are judgments that are rooted in philosophical questions that I hope to explain as we progress.

The paper will consist of three parts. The first part will be to explain the problem, as I see it, which I express as a modern paradigm. The second part will explain how the paradigm has permeated Western Culture and how it manifests itself. And the third part will offer present challenges to this paradigm.

The Problem as I See It

Like many others in the West, I went through the public education system where I learned about the wonders of science and how the scientific method has produced the miracles of technology that so define our modern civilization. Through this method of systematically counting, weighing, and measuring data, which has characterized natural science since the 17th century, the world has been blessed with the benefits of subduing and taking dominion over it. The fruits of these efforts have produced technologies that have often been described as ingenious, with the effect of awe and wonder, and indeed, considered "miraculous." The achievements of science and this method for acquiring knowledge about the world, have often been placed in contrast to the traditionally received authority in the West, such as the Christian Church. The difference between them, of course, is that the "miracles of science" can be empirically verified and duplicated and the biblical miracles cannot.

As a young student, I began to see that these products of science were only one aspect of an apparent larger divide between science and what I understood to be religion. Science seemed to be offering a view of the world that was in conflict with a so-called religious view of the world. This contrast, which is often depicted as a tension between science and religion, has extended beyond just miracles, and touches only the surface of the much deeper epistemological issue of knowledge v. opinion.

The question then that is often raised and was raised in my mind—is science based on knowledge and is religion based only on opinion? This led me to an even bigger question, can one view be rationally justified, or proven, and therefore claim knowledge? In other words, can one view prove its case to be the only rationally justified worldview? To wrestle with this issue would also include exposing the implications relating to questions regarding truth and error, knowledge and opinion, faith and reason. These are epistemological issues (philosophy, knowledge), and will be explored and, hopefully, convincingly answered in this short paper or in my book.

Were these views on religion and science actually at odds with each other—was one true and the other false—or was something else going on? How were these apparent tensions to be understood and resolved? I turned to philosophy to help me understand. And after many, many years, I was finally able to gather my thoughts in, *Religion and Science: Deconstructing a Modern Paradigm*, which addresses the issues at hand. In this book I consider the relationship between what is called religion and what is called science. What is the best way to understand it? I argue that the fundamental issue that divides the two views is an epistemological one. That is, judgements and beliefs about what can be known about the nature of reality at the most basic level, are presupposed by both religion and science and are not only different, but in fact contradictory. It then logically follows that two belief systems with contradictory foundational beliefs about the nature of the universe, are going to be at odds with each other. My book, then, essentially unpacks, critiques, and deconstructs the divide between these two categories of religion and science. It exposes the misleading way that the relationship has been taught, understood, and received by successive generations; which I call a "modern paradigm."

So, what is this modern paradigm that needs to be deconstructed? Simply stated, it is the general belief that what is popularly understood as science is based upon Reason, facts, and knowledge; it is objective, neutral, open-minded, it focuses on this world, and is relevant for commerce, education, and politics. The popular idea of religion is that it is based upon faith, feelings, personal values, morality, opinion, is subjective, biased, narrow-minded, focuses on a future world, irrelevant for commerce, education, and politics.

I also argue that this paradigm, as presently conceived, is a fabrication of Western modernity—particularly through the 19th and 20th centuries. Modernity has divided the world's belief systems in such a way that favors a naturalistic worldview, which is perceived as the rational view, against non-naturalistic worldviews that are perceived as non-rational. Modernity's development of science has defined religion to satisfy its purposes making the two categories unavoidably related, but mutually exclusive.

So, as a deconstruction project, I will demonstrate how modernity has erroneously produced its particular understanding of the term religion and for what purpose. Once assessed, the idea of science will be shown to be embedded in a belief system, a worldview, that has been established on a foundational belief that cannot be rationally defended. Additionally, the present conception of religion is unacceptable. So as a construction project, I will offer a new approach to dividing the world's belief systems. I will deconstruct, then reconstruct. Thus, intellectual progress through growth in knowledge and understanding will result.

This Paradigm is Culturally Promoted and Perpetuated

After many years of teaching Philosophy, Philosophy of Religion, and World Religions at the college level, I have become convinced that the dichotomy between a religious perspective, or worldview, and a non-religious one is deeply-seated in the Western consciousness. The religious and non-religious categories are often characterized by the religion and science model. Many students enter the classroom assuming this generally accepted divide and perceive a tension between them. They tend to insist that a 'scientific view,' is a valid and justifiable alternative to a religious view.

In keeping with the popular understanding, students consistently present the scientific view as the non-religious view—the neutral, publicly held view. I hear this comment from time to time from students—I'm not religious, I'm a person of science. This kind of comment is not surprising, it is the popular understanding. My response is, "that's good, can you defend that view?"

Over the last one hundred years or so, religious studies have flourished in the educational institutions of the West. The idea of religion, once the exclusive domain of Christian thinkers and believers, has now expanded to include a multitude of diverse belief systems and practices. Much of the dialogue in the academy today continues to focus on questions relating to theories of religion such as; what is it? why is it? can it be defined? and how does it relate to science? Thus, continuing the paradigm—the divide.

While these kinds of questions may be important, I approach the topic from a different perspective. Due to the tension that has developed between the idea of religion and non-religion, particularly in light of science and claims to exclusive knowledge, a different and more clear approach is necessary. I offer an alternative scheme that provides a more plausible way to divide the world's belief systems. And as a bi-product of the discussion, I also question and challenge the validity of the term, religion, as it is popularly used today.

That there is such a thing as 'religion' in the world, however, few would deny. Everyone today, at least in the West, seems to know what religion is and what it is not. A familiar account is that religion can be best explained as a certain set of beliefs, rules, and practices for living. It is typically thought to be belief in a transcendent reality, one that is not part of this material world, one that is holy, or sacred, and makes certain things in this world holy or sacred.

The idea of religion consists of performing particular rituals at particular times and it is often thought to be a belief in a higher power, a God or gods. Additionally, the idea of religion is thought to be a set of beliefs that interpret and explain life and, by implication, the nature of ultimate reality. To believe in this type of transcendent reality and to perform the corresponding prescribed behaviors or rituals, is to be religious, so the typical account goes.

We in the West commonly use the term religion freely, and assume that everyone knows what we are talking about. We refer to Christianity, Judaism, Islam, and Buddhism, for example, as religions and the adherents of these as those who are religious. There are the faithful, those who follow their religion more or less consciously and consistently, there are those who are somewhat religious, and, of course, there are those who have no religion at all. The common understanding seems to be that there is religion and non-religion, religious people and non-religious people, and there are religious views and non-religious views. At what can be called the 'popular' level, the term religion, as I just summarized, appears to be clearly understood and can be differentiated using the descriptions that I mentioned from what it is not, thus producing two separate categories—religion and non-religion.

These two categories are evident in virtually every area of life. For instance, an average bookstore will have numerous book sections including one on religion. Historians speak of religious histories and news analysts report on the latest happenings in the religious world. Examples depicting religion as a distinct category are endless, thus establishing a type of 'belief paradigm'—religion and non-religion—a particular way of looking at the world that has become a generally accepted conceptual scheme. These two categories have been received by the modern Western mindset and often without much critical thought. It's considered a given—that's what a paradigm is.

The idea of religion is thought by many scholars to be notoriously difficult to define, and is considered to be a particular bias based on faith or belief, personal feelings, or family tradition, and is not grounded in knowledge and facts. Put simply, a religious view, it is often said, lacks verifiable evidence and proof, but nonetheless is considered a tenable view by many. We could say that these views are fideistic, that is, beliefs held with no proof or rational justification. Those, then, who would affirm a religious view would be doing so based upon their personal opinion, or a blind faith, and not on proof or evidence. In this paradigm, it is believed that only beliefs that can

49

be empirically verified qualify for dialogue in the public square with all other beliefs to be considered private.

In keeping with the popular understanding, students consistently present the scientific view as the non-religious view—the neutral, publicly held view. Science is about the pursuit of neutral brute facts obtained through the use of reason and the scientific method, resulting in knowledge that can be publicly verified. The scientific view is commonly expressed as a naturalistic view, a materialistic conception of the universe—one in which only the physical, material world can be known with certainty. A non-material, or spiritual, realm is considered non-verifiable and, therefore, not based on science. Whether the spirit realm exists or not, is not knowable. This is such a common distinction that many identify themselves with one category or the other and often may feel antagonism from the other view. Critics, such as the contemporary group known as 'the new atheists,' express their disdain for religion and assert the need to abolish it favoring the idea of a world without religion—a totally, what is called, secular world.

In support of the scientific view, students will often make an immediate appeal to the voices of the leading lights of science, such as physicist Stephen Hawking's authoritative statement, "it is not necessary to invoke God to light the blue touch paper and set the universe going," or to biologist Richard Dawkins' general thesis, "the factual premise of religion—the God hypothesis—is untenable."[3] While many students tend to be accepting of alternative views to science, some are less tolerant and have other favorite authoritative figures like Sam Harris and Victor Stenger to whom they appeal. Science writer, Sam Harris, is a contributor to the perceived tension and intolerance between science and religion and sees a clash between them and expresses his disdain for religion when he says, "which of our present practices will appear most ridiculous from the point of view of those future generations that might yet survive the folly of the present? It is hard to imagine that our religious preoccupations will not top the list."[4] Physicist, Victor Stenger, when speaking of religion, makes a similar comment; Faith is absurd and dangerous and we look forward to the day, no matter how distant, when the human race finally abandons it. Reason is a noble substitute, proven by its success. Religion is an intellectual and moral sickness that cannot endure forever if we believe at all in human progress. [5]

This exclusively Western perceived distinction between religion and non-religion is oftentimes portrayed as facts v. opinion, or as knowledge (science) v. faith (religion). Western modernity has produced two categories of belief with these two entities, science and religion, as a common way to express them—the paradigm. But, why these two? A distinction has been made, but what are the essential differences between them that justifies the categories? Are there valid reasons for these categories and for the responses elicited by the scholars just mentioned, or are they what philosopher of science, Thomas Kuhn, calls a product of 'normal science,' a 'paradigm?' That is, as Kuhn explains, "achievements that some particular scientific community acknowledges for a time as supplying the foundation for its further practice."[6] The implication here is that the idea of normalcy is only temporary—for a particular time and context. While commitment to the same paradigm provides the basis for a consensus on particular research traditions, it is "sufficiently open-ended to leave all sorts of problems for the redefined group of practitioners to resolve."[7]

In a similar way, a paradigm has developed in modern history for how to understand the relationship between religion and science. The divide has become commonly accepted, but has issues that need to be more carefully examined and defined. Some of those problems are now coming to light and in need of closer critical assessment and resolution. This paradigm of modernity is flawed and needs to be deconstructed. My book identifies and responds to some of the tensions inherent in this current 'paradigm.' How are the two categories to be understood? Clearly, there is a history that has informed and produced these two ideas that have been, and continue to be, examined by anthropologists, sociologists, and historians for cultural significance.

Models for how to understand the historically developed relationship between science and religion have been devised and many books have been written to explain it. These models attempt to explain the relationship in terms of, spheres of knowledge, and how these spheres relate to each other, if at all.

The Modern Tension and Presuppositions

But my project is intended to be more than an historical assessment. The validity of the paradigm itself is critically examined and challenged. Differences between the ideas of science and religion at the most basic level are considered. It implements the insight of philosopher, Surrendra Gangadean, with his axiom, "[c]ritical thinking is by nature presuppositional; without the more basic in place, what comes after cannot be understood."[8] What is meant by this is that all humans think and have beliefs about various things. These beliefs are held together by reason and form a 'belief system' when focusing on a particular topic.[9] Some of the beliefs within the system are more basic than others. That is, what are considered less basic beliefs are dependent upon and are constructed upon more basic beliefs. Less basic beliefs are understood and derive their meaning in light of the beliefs that are more basic.

These most basic beliefs are considered foundational and are either explicitly or implicitly believed. For example, beliefs about what so-called religion is and does presuppose a more basic belief about the nature of reality. In other words, the idea of religion and how religion is expressed is embedded in one's larger view of the nature and purpose of the world, and how it works. The idea of religion is often thought to be about life's ultimate concerns and is understood in light of one's most basic belief about what ultimately exists. It addresses and provides answers to fundamental questions about the nature of existence. That ultimate belief then, informs one regarding choices that are considered good, or even *the greatest good*, that are helpful for people to understand and achieve the purpose and goal of life—to achieve a meaningful life.

The idea of religion is often thought to be about life's ultimate concerns and is understood in light of one's most basic belief about what ultimately exists.[10] It addresses and provides answers to fundamental questions about the nature of existence. That belief then, about what is ultimate, informs one regarding choices that are considered good, or even *the greatest good*, that are helpful for humans to understand and achieve the purpose and goal of life.

The idea of religion and the concerns associated with it can be expressed in the three traditional categories of philosophy. It is about beliefs concerning 'what is' (metaphysics), how that is known (epistemology), and how these beliefs are practiced in order to achieve 'the good' for human beings (ethics). The belief held in the area of metaphysics (what ultimately exists) serves as a foundational belief and is oftentimes not understood explicitly but is presupposed to be true. There is a systematic order to presuppositional critical thinking, from the more basic to the less basic. All human beings have beliefs and are held more or less consciously and consistently.[11] This is the case whether the beliefs are of a so-called religious nature or of a practical nature.

I address the issues through the lens of these philosophical categories, particularly epistemology, and how epistemological changes helped define Western modernity and ultimately produced the idea of religion. I show how changes in what qualified as knowledge produced the dichotomy in question and the resultant religion / science paradigm.

The Tension and Knowledge Claims

While the relationship between modernity, secularism, science, and religion is historically and culturally multi-faceted, it is important to keep in mind that my work focuses primarily on the epistemic component that produced the two belief categories—religion and science. That is, the significance of what qualifies as knowledge (and not opinion) will be explored as a major contributing factor in the development of the category distinction and the difference between them. Both categories claim 'to know,' however, that claim needs to be explored more fully and the meaning clarified.

It seems clear from my comments thus far, that, according to the popular understanding, science is based on reason and religion is not, it is often argued. This view of science has produced a perspective on the world that has come to be technically called, philosophical or metaphysical naturalism, a product of Western modernity with roots in classical Greek philosophy.[12]

It is important to note here that metaphysical naturalism is distinct from methodological naturalism. That is, metaphysical naturalism functions as the more basic belief, or philosophy of existence, that affirms that only a material world exists and then establishes methods that interpret all the data of science according to that basic belief. Methodological naturalism is the particular approach and set of assumptions used for gathering, interpreting, and understanding scientific data and presupposes metaphysical naturalism. Metaphysical naturalism functions as the more basic belief, or philosophy of existence, that affirms that only a material world exists and then employs methods that interpret all the data of science according to that basic belief.

Acquiring the Privileged Status

Due to the wide acceptance of this view, particularly in the Western academy, the notion that naturalism qualifies as the predominant, or privileged view, that is, the favorably accepted as true and therefore authoritative view of reality, is pervasive.[13] It is the basis for the favored method of inquiry by many classical as well as contemporary religion theorists.[14] As the authoritative view, scholars presuppose it to study the alternative 'religious' views and do their research in the 'science of religion' or the 'phenomenology of religion.' It is the function of reason and science to produce the proper understanding of alternative views that purportedly reject the authority of reason and the naturalistic view, and favor fideistic dogma and tradition. Thus, even though there may be uncertainty regarding how to define religion specifically, there appears to be a general consensus on what religion is and is not, which hinges on the use of reason and indicates the strength of the paradigm.

But how does one particular view attain a privileged status? There should be no doubt that the view grounded in reason and knowledge ought to be the preferred view and, as such, demands a type of privilege. There is no higher authority than reason itself. For rational human beings, to use reason consistently produces integrity and results in being human in the fullest sense. Reason and consistency also produce meaning. To use Dr. Gangadean's words, "persons as rational beings need meaning. Integrity, as a basic form of honesty, is a concern for consistency."[15]

When used properly, reason also produces knowledge, which then results in particular practices. Conversely, not to use reason consistently, or to hold beliefs without proof or evidence, would be to be devoid of knowledge and integrity. Privilege, then, simply means that the view established as the most rational has a perceived preeminence. To recognize this relationship, and in keeping with the

JOURNAL OF PUBLIC PHILOSOPHY

principles of modernity, is to recognize that knowledge, or the lack of it, has an ethical component as well. The ethical feature is evident in the famous quote by 19th C. English philosopher, W.K. Clifford (1845-1879), and a significant figure of enlightened modernity: "it is wrong always, everywhere, and for anyone, to believe anything upon insufficient evidence."[16] He refers to this as 'the ethics of belief.'

One's beliefs must be grounded in sound reasons and arguments—they must be rationally justified. Choices ought to be grounded in knowledge and not opinion. Modernity requires rational evidence as a necessary condition for belief as expressed earlier by naturalists, Hawking, Dawkins, and the others. The significance of these points is that there is a necessary relationship between belief, knowledge, and practice—the categories of philosophy.

Privileged Status and the Burden of Proof

As the privileged view in the Western academy, Naturalism is assumed to be 'true' and the owner of the exclusive research methodology, which is assumed to be neutral and objective. This point is evident by the questions that are asked. Due to its stronger position, science, or rather philosophical naturalism, assumes that the category of religion 'arises' and asks questions such as; where did religion come from, what is the nature of its origin, and why does it exist? In other words, what are the possible causes of views, such as theism, that reject naturalism? How and why is it possible, it is asked, for these alternative views to be believed?

These are the primary concerns of a naturalistic academic approach to religion theory, which assume a privileged role when asking these questions about opposing alternative views. That is, it assumes an authoritative role and perspective when interpreting and explaining other views. It also assumes the validity of the two categories of belief—there is naturalism and then there are the alternative views. From this it would appear that the idea of religion is any view that is contrary to naturalism. The academy is the place where critical thinking occurs, or ought to occur. And I would ask, should the academy not also be examining the uncritically held presuppositions, the foundational beliefs, of the privileged view?

Given the perspective of naturalism, the methods of inquiry by eminent religion theorists assume that the idea of religion is somehow derived from nature by natural causes; it is a thing and is explainable just as any other object of critical investigation. So-called religious belief systems are thought to be explainable in terms of either anthropology (E.B. Tylor), psychology (Freud), or sociology (Durkheim). Depending on the interests of the particular theorist, the specific answers to the questions will vary, however. These types of concerns, regularly raised in theory courses in university Religious Studies programs, presuppose a naturalistic perspective. Any affirmation of a reality that transcends a material reality is either dubious or a discoverable product of culture or a projection of the human psyche.

But in keeping with the questioning strategy, it can also be asked, where did this paradigm, this conceptual scheme, come from and why has this type of divide come to be so readily embraced in the West? Are these categories, as presently divided, warranted or is the divide just a thin veil for an Enlightenment ideal that gained favor in order to promote one view, naturalism, over the others? Why should naturalism not be considered just a modern social power construct?

To counter these charges, naturalism will need to provide rational proof for its most basic beliefs in order to maintain its privileged role. Without the support of a sound argument, could it be legitimately asked; from whence the origin of naturalism? Why does it exist and how did it arise? If religion arises, does naturalism also arise? The answer given for the origin question depends on the perspective of the questioner and the rational soundness of the respective position.

What About a Definition for the Terms, Religion and Science?

Religion scholars have struggled with this most challenging demand for definition and its place in intellectual inquiry. To grasp the essence of religion and for it to be a concept it must have specific characteristics that all members and only members of the class 'religion' have in common. This allows for the idea of religion to be differentiated from what it is not. It is at this point that comprehensive definitions have stumbled.

Consequently, many religion scholars accept that the term is undefinable and consider it simply a collective name, and opt for something like William James' view that religion, "consists in the belief that there is an unseen order, and that our supreme good lies in harmoniously adjusting ourselves thereto."[17] The difficulty here is that this expression is so broad that it could conceivably include all views, including naturalism. A naturalist may propose that "our supreme good lies in harmoniously adjusting ourselves" to the "unseen order" inherent in natural selection and the survival of the fittest. But if that is the intention of the statement, then the dichotomy between religion and non-religion would lose its meaning and dissolve. All views could be included in only one category, the religion category, or the non-religion category. If all is religion, then none is religion. But this, most likely, was not James' intention at all. However, an assertion like this when not clearly crafted loses its intended meaning.

But perhaps, it is not as difficult as it may at first appear. On the surface, to even speak of tension and separation seems odd if religion and science are understood in a straightforward manner. For instance, in a fundamental sense, religion, as I just explained, is often thought of as belief in the existence of a transcendent reality. It does not typically deny the existence of the physical world (in the West, but affirms a spiritual in addition to a material reality. Science, naturalism, on the other hand, also in a fundamental sense, consists of counting, weighing, and measuring the data gathered by exploring the physical world. Fundamentally, it is a descriptive and not a prescriptive process. For science, whether a transcendent reality exists or not, does not seem to be a primary concern for gathering data. The two appear to be complementary, as they were thought to be prior to the mid-nineteenth century. So why the separation and/or the tension? The tension arises at a different level, and in part, due to the ambiguity surrounding these two terms. It exists because the meaning and significance of the terms, religion and science, are embedded in a larger belief system, a worldview.

Worldviews provide the framework by which the data of experience and science are interpreted and explained. For meaning and significance, data needs to be interpreted—what does the data mean? As comprehensive views of the world are formed and adherents become more consciously aware of their own beliefs, the differences between one view and another become more apparent. The terms religion and science have been transformed from their original meanings as religio (piety) and Scientia (knowledge) and have become elements of comprehensive worldviews. They have become contextualized. Religion and science, as presently understood, are separated not because they are fundamentally antithetical to each other, but because they have become embedded in, and identified with, worldviews that interpret, and explain reality differently.

It should be apparent that what is called religion consists of various belief systems that can be understood, at least minimally, by what they believe to be true and by what they do. The common characteristic at the most basic level of the diverse views called religion, is that they all seek to make sense out of human experience. That is, they describe, interpret, and explain experience in order to maximize the meaning of it, and particular beliefs that form a system are what makes that happen.

It should also be clear that, similarly, naturalism is also a belief system that describes, interprets, and explains the nature of reality along with its various ways of practice and, therefore, also seeks to make sense out of human experience. The formal features, structure, and function of diverse belief systems are alike, but with different basic beliefs. That is, each belief system consists of, whether explicitly stated or uncritically presupposed, a metaphysic, an epistemology, and an ethic.

For science, the gathering of so-called 'neutral' data does not stop there, but includes more. To use the oft-quoted phrase, all data are theory-laden. Like religion, the additional component for science, or rather philosophical naturalism, is that of interpretation. Physical data alone are inconsequential—there is no meaning, and, therefore, must be incorporated into a larger framework that provides a basis from which to interpret the meaning and significance of the data.

So, at the level of basic belief, naturalism and the idea of religion are the same. As Dr. Gangadean explains it, "religion is the belief or set of beliefs one uses to give meaning to one's experience….since all give meaning to experience, all are religious." William James' attempt at definition, unwittingly, came to the same conclusion. All belief systems attempt to do the same thing. Once again, if all is religion, then none is religion. When understood in this way, the term 'religion' loses its distinctive and definitive characteristics and is, therefore, debatable whether it qualifies as a concept. It loses its meaning. All of the world's diverse belief systems then qualify as religion. Whether so-called religion or naturalism, belief systems are constructed for the purpose of giving meaning to existence. This includes determining the significance and meaning of data gathered from the physical world—what is typically called science.

Inherent in the respective systems are beliefs concerning the nature of ultimate reality, how that reality is known, and how life ought to be lived. Each has a different starting point. Each interprets and explains in light of its most basic judgment about what is ultimately real—a metaphysical judgment. Both are involved in interpretation, but affirm something different to be the most basic, or ultimate reality upon which the system rests.

Belief systems offer interpretations in the form of metanarratives, or grand stories, that explain the meaning and nature of the world and reality. Included in that interpretation is a view of the physical world and explanation of it. Hinduism, Christianity, and Darwinian evolution are examples of metanarratives.

The tension can now be framed as worldview v. worldview or theism v. philosophical naturalism. While the tension may not have been fully apparent by the mid-nineteenth century, as modernity matured and science transformed into a worldview based on philosophical naturalism, the separation and tension between the two perspectives became more pronounced. Awareness of metaphysical differences increased.

Recent Challenges to the Popular Paradigm

Naturalism, and its foundational belief that materialism is the only rational view, would not go unchallenged for long, however. Since the end of the 19thC. at least two epistemological challenges have been put forth. Both question the foundation upon which naturalism is constructed. The first challenges the very idea of a foundation for knowledge and translates into what has come to be known as postmodernity. The postmodern ethos, mostly expressed in the academic disciplines of the social sciences and humanities, has found itself at odds with the physical sciences, which still holds to a foundation. This tension came to a head in what was called the 'science wars' of the 1990's and is an on-going issue that is yet to be resolved. The second challenge retains a foundation, but challenges naturalism's particular foundational beliefs. I'll begin my comments with the first challenge.

As the twentieth century has clearly shown, naturalism has gained

JOURNAL OF PUBLIC PHILOSOPHY

predominance in the Western academy. Naturalism claimed Reason and verifiable evidence to make its case. As emphasized earlier, the fundamental issue between science and so-called religion is one of epistemology, how reality is known. Knowledge is the key here. Which view can claim knowledge and, therefore, truth? The modern outlook has been shaped by the quest for certitude, the absolutizing of the laws of nature (including reason), and the relegation of authority to the periphery, to mention just the major points.

The transition from the modern era to the postmodern can be understood as an epistemological revolution—a shift away from absolute knowledge and certainty. Theologian, Diogenes Allen, sees the present postmodern situation as "a massive intellectual revolution" where "the foundations of the modern world are collapsing" and "the principles forged during the Enlightenment...are crumbling."[18]

This revolution began with the maturation of naturalism and was represented by the philosophical pragmatism of Charles Sanders Peirce (1839-1914) and William James (1842-1910) of the early 20thC, and continued through the empiricism of Bertrand Russell, and Ludwig Wittgenstein (1889-1951), and finally to Willard Quine, Wilfrid Sellars, and Richard Rorty of the last half of the 20thC. Their line of empirically based epistemology has impacted and left its mark with implications for naturalism and its foundation. Pragmatic philosophy, a postmodern precursor, re-examined the Enlighten-ment's view of rationality. Pragmatism in philosophy undermined the prevailing Cartesian/Lockean tradition in three crucial areas, which represented the beginnings of nonfoundationalism as a philosophical criticism—that is, there can be no certain foundational belief upon which to build a belief system.

The first area of focus for this revolution was the rejection of Descartes' method of establishing the first principles, certainty, as a necessary introduction to philosophical inquiry itself. The second area was that the accepted metaphysics of understanding were rejected. That is, neither sense experience nor ideas were considered privileged as an authoritative basis of knowing. And thirdly, the rationalist or empiricist definition of truth as an isolated correspondence between self and world was also rejected. In its place was the understanding that truth is found in a social context of meaning shaped by the practical implications of ideas.

These three points became the basis for the skepticism and relativism of postmodernity. Postmodern thought has removed all bases for distinctions, such as the distinction between true and false, good and evil. No one view can claim to be true, right, or good. There is no rational basis for making these judgments. Choices are based on intuition, or feelings. For example, no sound argument is given for belief in God or belief in no God—only an appeal to like or dislike.

Building on the tradition of pragmatism, Quine, Sellars, and Rorty reject foundations of certitude, whether rationally or empirically determined, as the basis for knowledge in all types of theoretical thought. Philosophy, for Sellars, rather than being the discipline for determining objective truth, is "the reflective knowing one's way around in the scheme of things." Knowledge and Truth, in any objective sense, is not possible. Conceptual schemes, framed by 'culturally derived' sociology, psychology, economy, or history that have shaped and formulated traditions by which reality is defined, is what makes up the postmodern perspective. Human reason as the primary privileged capacity once considered able to discover knowledge of reality has been chastened and a more modest view of Reason has emerged.

In light of these twentieth century conclusions, it appears that naturalism has no rational basis, or proof, for claiming exclusive knowledge. It cannot be proven that matter is all that exists or that it is eternal, the foundational belief of naturalism. If nothing is clear, skepticism and nihilism then prevail. At best, it can only claim contextual, circular, consistency. Naturalism, then, is only one view among many, incommensurate with all others, and unable to claim truth and, therefore, privilege. Epistemological relativism, rooted in skepticism, allows all views to have their day. None can be determined to be right or wrong, true or false, good or evil.

The postmodern ethos has removed, at least theoretically, the ostensible conflict between science and religion. The popular paradigm and dichotomy collapse due to lack of evidence on each side. If there is no rational proof to favor the God hypothesis, what rational proof is there, then, to favor the matter only hypothesis? Why should one view be believed rather than the other? How, then, can naturalism justify its claim to exclusivity? The privileged view has been reduced to feelings and power. But whose feelings and whose power qualifies as the authority?

Additionally, the implications of applied postmodernity can be, arguably, culturally detrimental. As I just noted, with no rational basis for making distinctions, then choices, whether individually or culturally, lose their meaning and significance. All perspectives on reality are of equal value. If all choices are ultimately of equal value then they are equally meaningful. If all choices are equally meaningful then they are all equally meaningless. How do cultures survive when faced with a relativistic, meaningless existence—when all views are believed to be of equal value?

The main concern for this essay, then, is raised again—can naturalism's foundational belief that only a material reality exists for certain, be considered knowledge? According to the leading twentieth century critical thinkers, it may be proposed, but cannot be considered a universal certainty, rather, only contextualized 'opinions.' If this is the case, how then does naturalism qualify as the privileged view? Is there any reason to believe the inherited paradigm?

Challenge #2

The second challenge comes from philosophers who maintain that postmodernity and its coherentist epistemology is flawed. They argue that a foundation is necessary for knowledge, but would challenge the basic beliefs of Naturalism. They would argue that the claim that matter is all that exists and has always existed cannot be rationally justified—it cannot be proven, and therefore cannot claim knowledge. If knowledge is to be salvaged, then the strong challenges of Naturalism and postmodernity must be overcome beginning with the nature of Reason and its ability to produce knowledge. To reconstruct a foundation for knowledge, two obstacles will need to be overcome.

First, the limitations placed on Reason need to be removed. Reason then becomes the exclusive tool of inquiry and judgment, and common ground for discourse. Second, it must be demonstrated that certainty is possible. That is, a basic belief that is non-falsifiable. If the certainty of basic beliefs can be established, then less basic beliefs can be inferentially deduced. Once these objectives are accomplished, a foundation for thought that enables distinctions to be made will then establish clarity between opposing belief systems (worldviews).

First, Reason's limitations. What is needed is a response to the postmodern mentality of limited, or chastened Reason incapable of absolute, universal judgments on a normative reality. How, then, is Reason established as normative? To begin, Reason is used by all who think to postulate everything that is thought. It can be used incorrectly, but not denied without using it. It is self-evident that we think. It is also self-evident that we use the laws of thought—logic, or Reason. If Reason is denied then intelligent thought ceases. Even to say that Reason is limited is to make a judgment using Reason. Apparently, for postmoderns, Reason is capable of recognizing the idea of a transcendent reality, but not able to postulate anything meaningful

65

about it. Reason is the only light human beings have to dispel the darkness.

My first college philosophy Professor, Surrendra Gangadean, says this about reason:

> *Reason is transcendental. It is authoritative. It stands above all thinking and makes thinking possible. It cannot be questioned for it makes questioning possible. It is self-attesting. It testifies to itself and cannot be testified to by another. It is the highest authority in the realm of human knowledge. The deliverances of prophets, poets, philosophers, and physicists must be in accord with reason.* [19]

With these statements, reason is established as common ground for all who think. To be human is to use reason. Thinkers use the laws of reason—the laws of thought. To violate a law of thought, such as the law of non-contradiction, is to reduce a proposition to meaninglessness. If a proposition contains a contradiction, then it cannot be determined to be true or false—it is meaningless. The proposition must be understood before a judgment can be made. It could be said, therefore, that meaning is more basic than truth and reason is the test for meaning—something that my first philosophy professor taught me. A belief system must not be constructed on a contradiction nor contain contradictions in order to avoid meaninglessness. Reason, then, as the test for meaning, must, therefore, be the ultimate authority in matters of knowledge and truth.

But can reason produce the certainty required for a foundational basic belief? If so, then how? The first task for reason then is to produce a first principle of knowledge that can be considered certain. Since all worldviews agree that reason is used and is significant, the issue of differences and where to start the reasoning process is the fundamental concern that remains to be answered. Each presupposes a different self-evident first principle, or set of principles, from which to begin. Which one is right?

Twentieth century postmoderns have argued that there is no determinable starting point for the reasoning process because there are no first principles that can be granted the status of certainty. There is no foundational certainty that establishes a beginning point from which inferences can be deduced.

It is apparent that what is fundamentally at stake with the various belief systems is the issue regarding what ultimately exists. That is, the world as we experience it seems to be temporal, to change and pass away. All that exists seems to be dependent upon something else for its existence. Since something continues to exist, there must, then, be something that exists that is self-sustaining; it does not change or pass away—something that does not die, but has life in itself. There must be something that is eternal and the cause of temporal existence.

Naturalism claims that that something is the material world. It claims that only matter exists and is eternal. The material world, then, if eternal, would need to be self-sustaining and self-maintaining. However, two additional alternative views regarding existence and eternality need to be considered in addition to materialism. The first alternative view is that 'nothing' exists eternally and the second alternative is that only 'some' that exists is eternal (and some is not eternal). So this makes three options regarding existence and eternality; 1.) the view of naturalism—all that exists has always existed, 2.) nothing has always existed, 3.) the view of theism—only some that exists has always existed. These options have been explained in detail by, Surrendra Gangadean, in his work, *Philosophical Foundation*.

All worldviews (religions and philosophical naturalism) presuppose, explicitly or implicitly, one of these most basic beliefs about what exists ultimately. To divide the world's belief systems in this way is to reveal their differences at the most basic level. The common way of dividing the world's belief systems has been to use the natural/supernatural, or even the spirit/non-spirit models—as expressed by the popular paradigm. However, when discussing existence, the eternal/temporal distinction is more basic than the natural/supernatural or spirit/non-spirit distinctions and therefore more clear.

But before it can be determined what is eternal it must first be determined if it is possible to know that something is in fact eternal. Contrary to postmodern criticism, the human mind can have knowledge about what ultimately exists and certainty can be secured at the most basic and foundational level of thought. There must, of logical necessity, be something eternal and it can be shown to be the case. The opposite, of course (and contradictory), is that nothing is eternal. But if nothing is eternal, then what exists now would have had to have come into existence from non-existence (nothingness). To affirm this presents a contradiction and cannot therefore be true.

With two contradictory propositions such as 'nothing' is eternal contrasted to 'something' is eternal, the two cannot both be true and they cannot both be false. With a contradiction one proposition is true and the other, of rational necessity, is false. A rational argument is then necessary to show which is true and which is false. If it can be demonstrated that 'nothing is eternal' is logically impossible, then its opposite 'something is eternal' must, of necessity, be true. Gangadean sets up a logical proof as follows: Proof that there must be something eternal—our most basic belief.

1. Contradictory statements cannot both be true and cannot both be false.
   2. The contradiction of "some is eternal" is "none is eternal."
   3. If "none is eternal" then:
All is temporal.
All had a beginning.
All came into being.
   4. If all came into being then being came into existence from non-being.
   5. Being from non-being is not possible.
   6. Therefore the original "none is eternal" is not possible.

7. Therefore its contradiction "some is eternal" must be true.[20]

It is clear, Dr. Gangadean argues, that "through the use of reason, something must be eternal. For a skeptic to doubt this is to give up reason. To give up reason is to give up meaning and dialogue. 'There must be something eternal' is maximally clear since the opposite is not logically possible."[21]

Contrary to a major tenet of postmodernity, knowledge of something being ultimate can be grasped through the use of reason, as illustrated by this proof. Knowledge is possible. And, it is possible at the most basic level. Existence is our most basic concept. All other beliefs are less basic and derived from our most basic belief regarding existence. We do have certainty that something must be eternal, which is our most basic concept and whether consciously or unconsciously held is our most basic belief. Using Reason to obtain certainty is the beginning, the first step, to reconstructing a foundation for knowledge.

Naturalism's Response

When speaking of an eternal being, a being with no beginning and no end, theologians have historically used the term aseity—a being with attributes that include self-existence, self-maintenance, and independence with life in itself. Naturalists apply these same attributes to matter. Matter must minimally be self-maintaining in order to be eternal (no beginning or end. In order for naturalism to be true, it must be demonstrated that matter is self-maintaining. Can matter be demonstrated to be self-maintaining? In other words, taking an example from cosmology, once the sun and other stars consume their fuel can these burned out entities reconstitute themselves? This would be necessary for a material universe to sustain itself.

Physicists, however, have discovered an aspect of the second law of thermodynamics that prevents this from happening. As an example, the burning of fuel constitutes an irreversible process called entropy. Representing the consensus on this, renowned British physicist and ASU professor, Paul Davies, states the problem this way in his book, *The Mind of God: The Scientific Basis for a Rational World:*

> *At the heart of thermodynamics lies the second law, which forbids heat to flow spontaneously from cold to hot bodies, while allowing it to flow from hot to cold. This law is therefore not reversible: it imprints upon the universe an arrow of time, pointing the way of unidirectional change. Scientists were quick to draw the conclusion that the universe is engaged in a one-way slide toward a state of thermodynamic equilibrium. This tendency toward uniformity, wherein temperatures even out and the universe settles into a stable state, became known as the 'heat death.' It represents a state of maximum molecular disorder, or entropy. The fact that the universe has not yet so died—that is, it is still in a state of less-than-maximum entropy—implies that it cannot have endured for all eternity.[22]*

It would seem that due to entropy, as Davies' statement indicates, the material world and, indeed, the entire cosmos, is not self-maintaining. If it is not self-maintaining, then what enables it to continue useful existence after its 'heat death'? What regenerates it? And more importantly, the more basic question, what caused it to exist in the first place? Naturalists have precluded any non-natural cause for the existence of the cosmos, and of entropy, so must produce a natural explanation for its existence. Recognizing the inherent difficulties that entropy poses, physicists have sought an alternative approach to the issues of self-maintenance and origins. Appealing to Davies again he offers this explanation:

> *By weakening the link between cause and effect, quantum*

mechanics provides a subtle way for us to circumvent the origin-of-the-universe problem. If a way can be found to permit the universe to come into existence from nothing as the result of a quantum fluctuation, then no laws of physics would be violated. In other words, viewed through the eyes of a quantum physicist, the spontaneous appearance of a universe is not such a surprise, because physical objects are spontaneously appearing all the time—without well-defined causes—in the quantum microworld. The quantum physicist need no more appeal to a supernatural act to bring the universe into being than to explain why a radioactive nucleus decayed when it did.[23]

While Davies, as well as others, suggests that it may be possible to explain existence from nothing without violating the laws of physics, circumventing the laws of logic may be a bit more difficult. His proposition is the same as affirming existence from non-existence, being from non-being, 'a' from 'non-a,' which amounts to affirming a contradiction. To affirm a contradiction is to propose that something can exist and not exist at the same time and in the same sense. The question could be asked, what then is the difference between existence and non-existence? Davies uses reason to formulate his proposition, but then denies the laws of reason rendering it a meaningless proposition.

How can a meaningless proposition be understood or be determined to be true or false? A proposition built upon a contradiction must be false. He also suggests a "weakening" of the link between cause and effect and the appearance of objects "without-well-defined causes." It is not exactly clear what Davies is arguing for here. Not 'knowing' the cause is not, 'no' cause. Uncaused events are not logically possible and if a law of thought is violated then the proposition is meaningless and, therefore, false.

Dr. Gangadean addresses this crucial issue when he says:

If being from non-being were possibly true, then being would be no different from non-being. If being is no different from non-being then being is non-being, which is a contradiction. It violates the law of identity and the law of non-contradiction: something is both a and non-a in the same respect at the same time.[24]

Another proponent of existence from non-existence is ASU theoretical physicist, Lawrence Krauss. In his book, *A Universe from Nothing*, Krauss argues for why it is reasonable to believe "that getting something from nothing is not a problem."[25] The essential dilemma facing Krauss, and others holding this view, is that he asserts that what he is proposing is true and not false, but his system denies the possibility of distinctions. If existence cannot be distinguished from non-existence, a caused event indistinguishable from an uncaused event, and something indistinguishable from nothing, then how can true be distinguished from false? Meaning disintegrates and dialogue stops. Krauss touches on this when he says:

Why is there something rather than nothing?' must be understood in the context of a cosmos where the meaning of these words is not what it once was, and the very distinction between something and nothing has begun to disappear, where transitions between the two in different contexts are not only common, but required.[26]

While Krauss seems to recognize the logical difficulties with his shifting contexts, he is, nonetheless, arguing here that it is possible for nothing to produce something—for something to come into existence out of nothing without a cause—and not just an unknown cause. He is using semantics to make his argument. If "the very distinction between something and nothing has begun to disappear," then is the distinction between true and false also beginning to disappear? How can Krauss affirm his view to be true and not false? His words and distinctions are losing their meaning. Are we to maintain the distinction between true and false, but not between something and nothing?

In response to this proposition Dr. Gangadean clearly comments:

> *If being could come from non-being then there would be no distinction between being and non-being ("a" could then be "non-a"). If being could come from non-being then there could be uncaused events. There would be no way to distinguish a caused from an uncaused event. When basic distinctions collapse, all distinctions resting on them become meaningless.[27]*

Once again, when a contradiction is the foundation of a proposition then all intelligent dialogue ceases. A context of meaningless distinctions without differences quickly morphs into a context of nihilism. Reason as authoritative and a test for meaning is denied, and is contrary to a basic claim of naturalism—that it is the most reasonable position. With reason denied, where do we turn, how can we know? How can we think? All of the data of science needs interpretation and Reason provides that.

Krauss' claim to a reasonable explanation of the data becomes meaningless. How can this position be believed and still maintain integrity? It cannot. If naturalism is to be considered true, then it must rationally justify its first principles. It must demonstrate that matter is all that exists and that it is eternal. This cannot be done. For matter to be eternal it must be self-maintaining and the second law of thermodynamics (entropy) demonstrates that it is not.

Naturalists have then opted for that which exists to come into existence from non-existence, which proves to be a contradiction (existence is non-existence, A is non-A). Naturalism cannot prove its most basic belief, its foundational belief, not logically nor empirically. How then can naturalism claim knowledge and privilege? It cannot. The dichotomy between philosophical naturalism and so-called religion collapses. Categories are significant and have a place in scholarly inquiry, but not as modernity and the current paradigm have formulated them.

In conclusion — I presented my case, that the two-category approach to the world's belief systems, commonly understood as religion and science, "the modern paradigm," is inadequate and needs to be deconstructed and reformulated. It's time for a 'paradigm shift.' All worldviews need to be assessed at the level of their most basic belief regarding existence. All worldviews make judgments about what ultimately exists—essentially, what is eternal. All worldviews interpret and explain existence. All worldviews need to be judged and divided by their most basic belief, and when that is done they do end up in two categories—that is, the universe has always existed or the universe came into existence by a Creator.

Some worldviews can't rationally justify their most basic belief, such as Naturalism, and therefore, have no basis for claiming to be the privileged view—the view grounded in Reason and knowledge. With that awareness, that realization, the modern paradigm collapses—the spell has been broken. I will close with the famous quote by Socrates, "the unexamined life is not worth living."

Rodney W. Tussing
    May 2019

Endnotes

[1] I borrowed the title for this paper from Daniel Dennett's book called, *Breaking the Spell: Religion as a Natural Phenomenon*. I will challenge Dennett's thesis in this work, that the idea of religion is a naturalistic phenomenon.

[2] Rodney W. Tussing, *Religion and Science: Deconstructing a Modern Paradigm* (Phoenix: Public Philosophy Press, 2019)

[3]Stephen Hawking and Leonard Mlodinow, *The Grand Design*(New York: Bantam Books, 2010) 180, and Richard Dawkins, *The God Delusion* (New York: Houghton Mifflin Co. 2006) 189.

[4]Sam Harris, *The End of Faith* (New York: W.W. Norton & Co., 2005) 48.

[5]Victor Stenger, *The New Atheists: Taking a Stand for Science and Reason* (New York: Prometheus Books, 2009) 244.

[6]Thomas Kuhn, *The Structure of Scientific Revolutions* (Chicago: University of Chicago Press, 1962) 10.

[7] Kuhn, *The Structure,*10.

[8]Surrendra Gangadean, *Philosophical Foundation: A Critical Analysis of Basic Beliefs* (Lanham: University Press of America, Inc., 2008) quoted from the preface.

[9]The idea of a 'belief system' here is intended to mean logically connected beliefs, a coherence of ideas, an affirmation that a proposition, or propositions about the existence, experience, meaning, and nature of the world are true (held individually or collectively), and are more or less consciously and consistently held. The idea of a belief system is essentially a 'worldview.' Sam Harris rightly recognizes the significance of beliefs when he says, "A Belief is a lever that, once pulled, moves almost everything else in a person's life. Are you a scientist? A liberal? A racist? These are merely species of belief in action. Your beliefs define your vision of the world; they dictate your behavior; they determine your emotional responses to other human beings." *End of Faith*, 12.

[10]Ivan Strenski, in his, *Thinking About Religion: An Historical Introduction to Theories of Religion,* addresses this point in his first chapter section on 'Natural Religion.' In it he states, "Those that adhered to the idea of Natural Religion typically felt that human beings therefore can *know* about ultimate truth by their own human abilities. Divine intervention is not required for people to know God, for example." (10). Here he seems to indicate that intellectual inquiry

on basic issues has, historically, been equated to the idea of religion. This, of course, assumes a particular definition of the term 'religion.' (Oxford: Blackwell Publishing, 2006). See also Roy Clouser's, *The Myth of Religious Neutrality* (Notre Dame, In., University of Notre Dame Press, 2005). In this work Clouser argues that religious belief is belief in anything with eternal attributes, that is "divine per se."

[11]Gangadean, *Philosophical Foundation*, 3.

[12]For the purposes of this work, naturalism, and more specifically philosophical or metaphysical naturalism, will be considered a 'world-view' similar to the definition in footnote 2 above. Chapter two of my book will explain how it came to be considered a worldview. The basic metaphysical beliefs of this view are something similar to William Drees' statement that "naturalism assumes that all objects around us, including ourselves, consist of the stuff described by chemists in the periodic table of the elements" and that theism is irrelevant. Drees also quotes an applicable comment by Charley Hardwick that further defines naturalism, "(1) that only the world of nature is real; (2) that nature is necessary in the sense of requiring no sufficient reason beyond itself to account for its origin or ontological ground; (3) that nature as a whole may be understood without appeal to any kind of intelligence or purposive agent; and (4) that all causes are natural causes so that every natural event is itself a product of other natural events." "Religious Naturalism and Science," in Clayton and Simpson, eds. *The Oxford Handbook of Religion and Science* (New York: Oxford University Press: 2006) 110. The term 'naturalism' is not intended to mean the same as it is used by J. Samuel Preus in his, *Explaining Religion: Criticism and Theory from Bodin to Freud* (Atlanta: Scholars Press, 1996) or in Russell McCutcheon's, *Manufacturing Religion* (New York: Oxford University Press, 1997). Both of these scholars view naturalism strictly as a method "to study religion as a part of human culture and history...without the benefit of clergy." *Manufacturing Religion*, ix.

The idea of modernity in this project will be delimited and understood primarily from an epistemological perspective. As such, the focus will be on the impact of changes between pre-modern, modern, and postmodern with respect to what qualifies as knowledge is explained in my book.

[13]See George Marsden's, *The Soul of the American University* (New York: Oxford University Press, 1994). In this work Marsden argues that today in the American University secular naturalism is generally perceived as the only valid academic perspective and precludes alternative perspectives.

[14]Including not only the classical religion theorists such as Hume, Durkheim, and Freud, but also contemporary theorists such as Pascal Boyer and Daniel Dennett.

[15]Gangadean, *Philosophical Foundation*, 143-148.

[16]W.K. Clifford, *The Ethics of Belief*, quoted in Steven Cahn, ed., *Ten Essential Texts in the Philosophy of Religion* (New York: Oxford University Press, 2005) 372.

[17]Quoted in Lewis Hopfe, Mark Woodward, *Religions of the World*, 8[th]ed. (Upper Saddle River, NJ: Prentiss-Hall, 2001) 5.

[18]Diogenes Allen, *Christian Belief in a Postmodern World: The Full Wealth of Conviction* (Louisville: Westminster/John Knox, 1989) 2

[19]Gangadean, *Philosophical Foundation*, 11

[20]Gangadean, *Philosophical Foundation*, 43

[21]Gangadean, *Philosophical Foundation*, 44

[22]Paul Davies, *The Mind of God: The Scientific Basis for a Rational World* (New York: Simon & Schuster, 1992) 47.

[23]Davies, *Mind of God*, 61-2.

[24]Gangadean, *Philosophical Foundation*, 45

[25]Lawrence Krauss, *A Universe From Nothing* (New York: Free Press, 2012) xiii.

[26]Krauss, *Universe,*182-3.

[27]Gangadean, *Philosophical Foundation*, 44.

Can Natural Law Theory be Rationally Justified?

Practical Ethics & the Backdoor Metaphysics of New Natural Law Theory

Mevin Joshi

In a 2015 article published in the *American Journal of Jurisprudence* by John Finnis titled, "Grounding Human Rights in Natural Law," Finnis responds to the main criticisms of the republication of a review written by Ernest Fortin (1982) against Finnis's seminal book, *Natural Law and Natural Rights*. The response by Finnis concerns a specific critique of "the freedom of thought and/or the intellectual autonomy and integrity of work within an intellectual tradition that overlaps with a 'faith tradition.'"[1] Finnis "shared Fortin's judgment that the neo-Thomism (ONLT) current in manuals and textbooks in the decades before 1965 was philosophically inauthentic."[2] Therefore, Finnis, an advocate of New Natural Law Theory (NNLT) first articulated by Germain Grisez in 1965, writes in his article of the tightly-held perpetual link between the possibility of Thomism being true with the plausibility of the re-articulated ethical system being sound. He hopes to make, or keep, Thomism relevant in contemporary academic and public discourse.[3]

The goal of this paper is to argue that Finnis's method results in a failure to recognize a metaphysical assumption shared by both ONLT and NNLT. Finnis's method involves the rejection and re-articulation of neo-scholastic Aristotelian-Thomistic Natural Law (ONLT) on behalf of NNLT, and the additional attempt to follow the 20th-century trend of practical philosophy to substantiate an inclusion within contemporary jurisprudence, politics, and ethics. Natural Law is the only hope for a universal objective law that directs us toward a common moral law suitable for a global community. However, the case made in this paper will be that ONLT and NNLT are unable to rationally justify the metaphysical absolute and therefore will not be successful to the end of Natural Law as the universal Moral Law. Natural law theory can be improved by understanding its metaphysical deficiencies and shifting the narrative to an understanding and approach that could complete the task of grounding the moral law.

Both natural law theories assume a view of the highest reality, which is not rationally justifiable through their respective approaches to natural law. I will show that to avoid this problem, NNLT attempts to bring in metaphysical assumptions through the backdoor as one of eight incommensurable goods that it purports to be universally self-evident. Furthermore, I will argue that for both ONLT and NNLT, the assumed view of what is ultimate reality is not clearly accessible through their versions of natural law, thus leading both views to a kind of metaphysical fideism. It is in this sense that there is no essential difference between NNLT and NL, classically understood, notwithstanding the shift in the NNLT view of metaphysics through the incommensurable good of religion. Therefore, for both these views, when consistently held, there can be no rational justification for the culpability of the actions of moral agents through these natural law theories themselves. Unless these problems are adequately addressed by finding the rationally justifiable (instead of plausible) approach to establish a metaphysical absolute through natural religion/law without appealing to the "grace perfects nature" narrative, the so-called natural law renaissance will become less germane among contemporary competing ethical theories and will not possess the grounds to become the global moral law.

Perusing through introductory ethics textbooks today, one will generally find at least four competing theories in play: utilitarianism, deontology, ethical egoism and virtue ethics, among a few ancillary others. The most notable motif these theories have in common is the focus on practical philosophy, which is primarily concerned with a pragmatic justification for morality disassociated with any attempt to rationally justify a metaphysical basis by which to deliberate (the default metaphysics and anthropology are evolutionary biology/non-cognitivism). Since the Enlightenment, renewed interest in practical philosophy transitioning into the latter half of the 20th century has brought with it a renaissance of natural law.

One of the primary reasons that natural law theory is receiving token attention in contemporary higher-education and culture is due to the handful of scholars in prominent positions of academia from the ilk of NNLT who have engaged in the so-called culture war where opposition to gay marriage and abortion have been center stage. Among the most notable are Grisez (recently deceased – formerly Georgetown University and emeritus Mount Saint Mary's), Finnis (recently retired – Oxford and Notre Dame), Joseph Boyle (recently deceased – University of Toronto), Robert George (Princeton University) and Christopher Tollefsen (University of South Carolina). The New Natural Law Theory (coined perhaps pejoratively by Old Natural Law proponent and NNLT's most ardent critic, Russell Hittinger, postulates that the theory's principles of practical reason are self-evident principles independent of any human psychology. It maintains that these principles are basic and specify human action and that people have intelligible reasons to pursue their well-being and the well-being of societies writ large. The practical reasonableness of these principles, according to Grisez, Finnis and their collaborators, cannot be reduced to purely instrumental purposes. I will elucidate the theory in a section below.

Origination, Collaboration, and Development

In this section, I will give a brief sketch of how Grisez, Finnis and their collaborators originated, developed and defended NNLT. I will explain two important reasons they give for the theory's development and its rejection of ONLT. The first reason is what has been called the Humean (David Hume) fact-value or is-ought gap, which states that moral obligations cannot be derived from facts about human nature. I will then expound upon the bifurcation of practical and theoretical/speculative reason in further understanding NNLT's position on knowledge.

To buttress their claim, New Natural Lawyers (NNLers) invoke a scriptural reference as a description of what is meant by Thomas Aquinas's first principle of practical reason (FPPR). Later, their position on practical reason will be used to give what they believe is a better, more effective (though not conclusive) argument for God's existence. Secondly, is Grisez's aberration from the beatific vision of ONLT. The Grisez-Finnis Theory rejects the neo-platonic element of neo-scholastic ONLT. The two points of rejection, if Grisez and Finnis are correct, show the shortcomings of ONLT. In a later section, I will provide Grisez's re-formulation of the beatific vision (sharing in the basic goods), which I will maintain is an antinomy from the neo-platonic version. The Grisez-Finnis argument still will not suffice, I will argue, to give a rational justification for a metaphysical absolute thereby undermining their project. (Please note that I use natural religion and natural law interchangeably throughout this essay).

The Is-Ought Gap

Working within the context of analytic jurisprudence and political philosophy, Finnis read:

> *[His] way into the natural law tradition...as a final-year law student and then during [his] doctoral studies, [he] was disconcerted by the inability or willingness of the modern writers to meet students where they are - equipped by school teachers and journalists with views derivative from Hume and Russell or other varieties of modern skepticism about good and bad, right and wrong in human action, and with scientistic determinism, materialism and conceptions (e.g. Logical Positivistic) of the limitations of reason. So [he] ought not to have been surprised, yet [he] was, at the inability or unwillingness of reviewers and other readers from the more or less Thomistic tradition to take into account the book's genre, and its primary intended audience."* [4]

This concern was a major impetus behind the content of Finnis's *Natural Law and Natural Rights*, which H.L.A. Hart chose as the title before commissioning it to Finnis at Oxford. Consequently, the resurgence of practical philosophy in the 20th century was a catalyst that engendered NNLT to procure a seat at the table of academic and public discourse. It was Grisez's interpretation of Thomas Aquinas's first principle of practical reason (FPPR) in the *Summa Theologica* that became the basis for Finnis's formulation of the theory. Finnis acknowledges Grisez for founding the theory and Grisez credits Finnis for providing its best philosophical development and presentation.[5]

The re-interpretation of classical natural law theory (rejecting the 17th-century neo-scholastic interpretation of Francisco Suarez) originated through Grisez in his 1965 commentary of Aquinas's FPPR in the *Summa Theologica*. Aquinas presents his FPPR as "good is to be done and pursued, and evil is to be avoided." The neo-scholastics, as they understood Aquinas, interpret 'good' as referring to morally binding acts and 'evil' as acts that do not conform to morality. Grisez's "main purpose" in his commentary was "not to contribute to the history of natural law, but to clarify Aquinas's idea of it (FPPR) for current thinking."[6]He concluded that, for Aquinas (contra Neo-Thomism), the normativity of the natural law is not deduced from any ontologically purported facts about human anthropology. Aquinas, as Grisez comprehends him, held that the FPPR is not morally binding. He argues that Aquinas considers the FPPR "to be a source, rather than a limit, of action."[7] Instead of a limit on action, Grisez understands Aquinas's FPPR to govern all, morally good or evil, practical deliberations. "Good," for Grisez, is not only morally good but also what is intelligibly worthwhile to pursue for any moral agent. "Evil" corresponds to any illegitimate treatment of the practical intelligible goods the Grisez-Finnis Theory holds are universal (more on this later). Robert George, a self-professed collaborator of NNLT, gives a helpful explication,

The work done by the first principle is more primitive. It states a condition of any coherent:

> *Practical thinking, viz., that one's reasoning be directed toward some end that is pursuable by human action. Even morally bad choices, to the extent that they are intelligible, meet this condition (although...not so well as morally upright choices). Consider, for example, a choice that mistreats another person. To the extent that such a choice has an intelligible point, it will be consistent with the first principle of practical reason, despite its immorality. Understood as a directive, the first principle is weak: It requires only coherence, not full moral rectitude.[8]*

For instance, the choice by the Mayans to provide human sacrifices for the constant burning of the sun would not be, according to Grisez's practical philosophy, unintelligible. Even though for NNLT, offering human sacrifices is universally immoral, it supports the thesis of the self-evident universality of the basic good of religion in all cultures.

Under the neo-scholastic interpretation of ONLT, as stated earlier, ethical normativity is embedded in, and derived from, human nature. By contrast, NNLT maintains that it is neither necessary nor sufficient to understand premises about human nature to understand the obligatory principles of natural law. As Finnis believes Aquinas to assert:

> As plainly as possible that the first principles of natural law, which specify the basic forms of good and evil and which can be adequately grasped by anyone of the age of reason (and not just by metaphysicians), are per se nota (self-evident and indemonstrable). They are not inferred from facts. They are not inferred from metaphysical propositions about human nature, or about the nature of good and evil, or about 'the function of a human being,' nor are they inferred from a teleological conception of nature or any other conception of nature. They are not inferred or derived from anything. They are underived (though not innate).[9]

In other words, one need not have in place that one is created in the image and likeness of the God of theism (which both old and new natural lawyers believe is correct). One need not believe that humans have a teleological purpose and destiny or, for that matter, that humans are the product of a macro-evolutionary process. {{In any case, NNLT does not hold that no anthropological knowledge unequivocally is necessary to know the FPPR}}. Finnis provides us with a further explanation:

84

...practical reasoning begins not by understanding this nature from the outside, as it were, by way of psychological anthropological or metaphysical observations and judgments defining human nature, but by experiencing one's nature, so to speak, from the inside, in the form of one's inclinations. However, again, there is no process of inference...by a simple act of non-inferential understanding one grasps that the object of the inclination which one experiences is an instance of a general form of good, for oneself (and others like one).[10]

Experiencing one's personal inclinations to pursue intelligible ends is per se nota and self-evident. Why? It is because everyone self-evidently practices these goods. Experiencing one's nature from the inside is sufficient, as the NNLers see it, to understand what is good and hence what ought to be pursued. To act is to be directed. To find out the way the world is (doing metaphysics) is not directive. Whereas theoretical work comes to an end with an answer, practical work comes to an end with action. Under Finnis's interpretation, "for Aquinas, the way to discover what is morally right (virtue) and wrong (vice) is to ask, not what is in accordance with human nature, but what is reasonable. And this quest will eventually bring one back to the underived first principles of practical reasonableness, principles which make no reference to human nature, but only to human good." [11] Human good refers to the intelligible ends which will bring about individual and communal flourishing.

Finnis believes that the practical and theoretical distinction which, according to him, is found in ONLT perfectly corresponds to the modern distinction.[12] In fact, if Finnis is correct, then the Humean is-ought gap is a red herring against natural law correctly understood. Since, for NNLT, the FPPR is self-evident and therefore not deduced from anthropological and metaphysical speculation, there is no precondition to know the self-evident truths of FPPR. It is important to note, again, that although Finnis does hold to an ontological connection between human nature and obligation,[13]the FPPR and moral norms are not epistemologically derivable from human nature. [14] Put another way, the palpability of the FPPR is not derived from human nature, but instead, participation in it perfects human nature. Alternatively, perhaps even better stated, is presently perfecting human nature. For instance, according to NNLT, the perfecting of the nature of the reader of this paper is currently happening since the reader is participating in the incommensurable good of knowledge.

The Beatific Vision

The second major point of departure for NNLT is the beatific vision. Aquinas's beatific vision states that the ultimate end of human life is a direct contemplation of God the soul enjoys after physical death in a state of ecstasy. Continuing along the line of human nature being perfected, Aquinas believed that human nature is perfected as it participates in the divine essence of the beatific vision. Whereas the NNLers view knowledge as continuing and inexhaustible, Aquinas viewed the finite ontological aspect of humans as possessing knowledge that will not continue to grow in the beatific vision. Although knowledge, for the NNLers, is limited, nevertheless, it continues to grow while never attaining all knowledge. Here Grisez assails Aquinas for being blinded by his synthesis of Aristotle and his affinity for the neo-Platonism found in Augustine:

> Aquinas was carrying out a large project of synthesis between Aristotle's thought and previous Christian theology, especially that of St. Augustine. The points of which the two more or less agreed led Aquinas to a view of beatitude that he felt certain was right: beatitude was the true ultimate good to be intended by a human agent in every choice (Aristotle) which would completely

satisfy the human person's restless heart (Augustine). On that view, of the true ultimate end, nobody simultaneously could intend both it and some other ultimate end. Aquinas was certain about the conclusion his argument needed to reach, and such certainty can distract even the best mind from obvious data that would falsify it.[15]

A fundamental contributing factor for Aquinas's beatific vision was his carrying out of Aristotle's empiricist epistemology, which Aquinas himself adopted. "Our knowledge takes its beginning from sense. Hence our natural knowledge can go as far as sensible things can lead it. But our mind cannot be led by sense so far as to see the essence of God, because sensible effects of God do not equate the power of God as their cause. Hence from the knowledge of sensible things the whole power of God cannot be known; nor therefore can His essence be seen." *(Summa Theologica* 58 1, Q. 12, A. 12).

For Aquinas, the essence of God can only be known when the soul leaves the body. Together with Aristotle's metaphysics, Aquinas gives his famous Five Ways, all of which do not conclusively prove the existence of the God of Christian theism.[16] It follows that ONLT's epistemology and natural religion (leading to the beatific vision) do not succeed in grounding ethics on a rationally justifiable metaphysical absolute as the basis for moral culpability. If the existence of God cannot be known while in the body, then how could there be the rational justification for ethics (natural law) in this bodily life? The NNLers rightly criticize ONLT on this point.

The beatific vision "downgrades most of the specifically human goods" for which people intelligibly hope.[17] Not only that but also if ONLT's view of the beatific vision is the end of humankind, then what effect does that have on the rational justification of ethics in this world for those who do not sympathize with ONLT's ethical interpretive framework? It is not rationally justifiable over and against other positions. NNLT rejects both the anthropological (natural law based on human nature and metaphysical approaches of ONLT, and in place of the two, relocates ethics on its version of practical philosophy. "...theoretical reflection on the virtues is far less helpful than practical reflection" on decisions by moral agents to consider their moral plight and responsibility to "find God's plan for their lives, accept that plan, living according to it..."[18] The response given by NNLT becomes this-worldly focused while bringing in metaphysics through the back end. Even granting that an 'is' cannot be derived from an 'ought,' and the insufficiency of the beatific vision to understand the relevance of the goods of this world, how does it help that the Grisez-Finnis metaphysical claims are less dubious? If morality is not derived from human nature, how do the NNLers attempt to rationally justify their ethical claims? How can they hold to an epistemologically unjustified theistic anthropology through natural law, and yet believe there is an ontological relationship between human nature and morality? Moreover, what are these intelligibly worthwhile self-evident universal goods? The next section will explain how the good of religion is included in NNLT as one of eight incommensurable intelligible goods.

The FPPR and Incommensurability Thesis

Every theory proposes some self-evident premise. Building on Grisez's critique of ONLT, Grisez, Finnis and their collaborators identify these intelligibly worthwhile goods as self-evident and pre-moral. As the laws of logic are self-evident in a theoretical sense, these eight universal goods worth pursuing are self-evident in a practical sense. The self-evident, per se nota goods, are more or less as follows:
  1) Life and Health
  2) Knowledge and Aesthetic Experience
  3) Excellence in Work and Play

4) Peace with others, Justice, Neighborliness, Friendship, Sociability

5) Harmony as opposed to inner conflict – the inner peace of a morally mature and

well-integrated person

6) Practical Reasonableness and Consistency between one's self and its expression

7) Marriage and its fulfillment by parenthood

8) Reconciliation and Friendship with God that religion seeks (Transcendence that may

or may not be)

There is no hierarchy within the above list, and thus they are considered irreducible and incommensurable. (Neither does it appear to be much different from the eight-fold path of Buddhism). Every action, for NNLT, is motivated by a fundamental good. Practical rationality is operating when it pursues one or more of the essential human goods. They do not arise from any supposedly more fundamental good. A satisfaction of desire is not a basic good. The basic goods are pre-moral in that they do not presuppose any moral judgment. They are structured as the basis for any human society to lastingly function, not for mere survival, but for integral human fulfillment. Our clear grasp of human goods makes moral evaluation possible.

Morality, for NNLT, is derived from the first principle of morality (FPM) through the per se nota self-evident goods. Finnis explains, "In voluntary acting for human goods and avoiding what is opposed to them, one ought to choose and otherwise will those and only those possibilities whose willing is compatible with integral human fulfillment. It is a guiding ideal rather than a realizable goal."[19] It means that one should not act against any of the incommensurable goods thereby curtailing integral human fulfillment or the common good for human flourishing. Acting against the common good or integral human fulfillment is immoral because it will not promote human flourishing. Note that the FPM does not justify acting. It only facilitates the correlation of the reasons presented by the pre-moral irreducible basic goods and permits practical reasonableness. Not all practical (self-evident) knowledge is moral knowledge, though all moral knowledge is practical knowledge.

For this paper, a comprehensive explanation and critique of the FPPR and FPM is not inherently conducive. Our aim here is to understand how the good of religion fits into the scheme of NNLT. With the final basic good of NNLT being religion, it is "an irreducibly distinct form of order."[20] However, the good of religion has conflicted with the view that denies the knowledge of a transcendent order of things bearing on moral agency since the time of the enlightenment challenges against any successful program of natural religion. Hittinger makes an insightful assessment: "The problem is cast in Kantian terms. Lacking metaphysical, empirical, or historical evidence to demonstrate the existence of a transcendent order, much less a personal God, one is indeed faced with the problem of affirming the good of religion."[21] On the other hand, the problem for Hittinger and the old natural lawyers is that the enlightenment challenges precisely reject the metaphysical stance of ONLT, which is rightly criticized by Grisez. Although Finnis, unlike Grisez, does not take us into moral theology, he and Grisez share the same philosophical assumption. "The good of religion is in fact realized whenever one must choose between what is right and wrong and chooses what is right."[22] It is ultimately understood as grounded in, and open to, harmony with the Grisez-Finnis transcendent source, which presupposes that persons are living according to the eight incommensurable goods.

The good of religion "is a response to eudaimonistic questions about the unity and transcendent significance of the moral life as a whole."[23] The distinction between eudaimonistic claims about the meaning of life and normative claims about moral agency in NNLT are entrenched in the good of religion and should not be confused with one another. NNLT universally affirms that religion plays a transcendent normative role; that all cultures have a sense of being in good harmony with a transcendent source. However, the theory also holds that the ultimate meaning of life, based on the irreducibility of the pre-moral goods, is best explained abductively via Christian revelation, which will be discussed further later.

It is not as though the NNLers have attempted to avoid metaphysics. In a 1987 article in the American Journal of Jurisprudence, Grisez, Boyle, and Finnis do mention their metaphysical affiliations:

> *As a theory of some of the principles of human action, what we offer here presupposes many theses of metaphysics and philosophical anthropology – for example, that human intelligence is irreducible to material realities, that doing and making are irreducible to one another, that human persons and their actions are caused by an uncaused cause, and so on. We defend many such presuppositions elsewhere.[24]*

For theists such as the NNLers, God is not Plato's Demiurge or Aristotle's Unmoved Mover or Advaita's Brahman. Nor is God an impersonal ground of being in the Tillichian (Paul Tillich) sense. In a repeated lecture given by George at various speaking engagements, he offers a scriptural reference from Romans 2:14-15: "For when Gentiles who do not have the Law do instinctively the things of the Law, these, not having the Law, are a law to themselves, in that they show the work of the Law written in their hearts, their conscience bearing witness and their thoughts alternately accusing or else defending them" (New American Standard Bible). As Grisez, Finnis and their collaborators understand Paul the Apostle, the directiveness of the FPPR is congruent with NNLT that non-theists who do not possess the Mosaic Law or theistic metaphysical beliefs, still, in fact, do what the law directs them to do. It is self-evident and undeniable that all humans do NNLT's eight incommensurable goods, according to NNLT.

If the public discourse of the Grisez-Finnis Theory can begin on the terms where their intelligible goods are agreed upon as the per se nota common ground, then, for Grisez, Finnis and their collaborators, much headway can be made in the broader context of practical philosophy, and in particular, universal normativity to bring in religio-metaphysical considerations through the back door. The theory's beginning is not a hypothesis, but rather a pragmatic justification based on a descriptive analysis to track how people act and think. It is continuing in the same line of thought as 20th-century practical philosophy void of giving weight to a metaphysical justification at the forefront of their theory. Although Grisez, Finnis and their collaborators rightly criticize the neo-Platonism of ONLT, they believe that natural religion cannot be rationally justified, and therefore appeal to Christian revelation. However, this begs the question.

NNLT stops short of claiming that all Ten Commandments are knowable through the natural law itself. If all Ten Commandments are rationally justifiable through the natural law, it follows that they are knowable by all theists and non-theists through the natural law. If it is knowable, then must there be epistemological, metaphysical and moral responsibility for disregarding it? For the NNLers, the Romans account of a natural law presupposes the existence of God the creator (Commandments 1-4), not just a moral law giver (Commandments 5-10). In an earlier section of the Romans account, as interpreted by many theists, was made the incredulous claim, for doubters, that not knowing the highest reality of the Decalogue (even without Mosaic and Christian revelation) renders moral agents theoretically and morally culpable.

In light of their view of understanding metaphysics via any natural religion, their direction is to take practical morality (a variation of cosmological contingency) to support their metaphysics. The result is to bring in the view of the highest reality through the back end. The lack of confidence the NNLers possess in natural religion stems from the fact that they have a low view of the Aristotelian-Thomistic (ONLT) approach to rationally justify a sound argument for the existence of

God. There is an explicit rejection of Aristotelian-Thomistic meta-physics and an implicit conceding to the enlightenment challenges of Hume and Kant of the limitations of reason. Grisez states that he does not believe one can get to the "unmoved mover and legitimately call it God" and criticizes Aquinas for following "Aristotle too far."[25] However, as Grisez sees it, "An argument is essential to establish the conclusion that God exists; to establish this conclusion is useful, not so much to prove it to persons who do not accept it as to establish a real referent for beliefs of those who do accept it."[26] Finnis, accordingly, states that we can get to an uncaused cause through natural religion, but not God the creator.[27]

If what Finnis concludes is true, the natural religion and natural law of both ONLT and NNLT do not succeed in establishing the rational justification for moral responsibility of a creator. In this sense, the old and new natural lawyers are not essentially different. Only the second half of the Decalogue can be known through the natural law, [28]because those commandments are what correspond to the self-evident practical principles hitherto entertained. The "Thou shall not" of the second half of the Decalogue seems to be the equivalence of "good is to be done, evil avoided" after the eight self-evident pre-moral goods are accepted. It is in line with the emphasis on practical ethics as the self-evident foundation to work back to a metaphysical highest reality that may or may not be[29]because it cannot be known through the natural law. Regarding Grisez, this is not surprising since in quoting arguably the most oft-quoted scriptural attempt at inferring theistic metaphysics (Romans 1:19-20), he omits "that they are without excuse" for not acknowledging the creator.[30] In place of Aquinas's archaic Five Ways, the Grisez-Finnis Theory purports that natural law or FPPR (practical reasonableness in pursuing the eight incommensurable goods) leads humanity to the ideal of integral communal fulfillment (ICF).

The ideal of ICF is most consistent, according to Grisez, with the Special Revelation account found in the book of Genesis.[31]NNLT's direction is validity, reasonability and therefore, plausibility, instead of culpability through the "things that are made." If the NNLers invoke the natural law Decalogue written in the hearts of all humans, and the Decalogue speaks of the highest reality, then there seems to be an inconsistency in the application of the initial premise that there is the highest reality found in the Decalogue, universally knowable through the natural law, apart from biblical revelation. Plausible justification is not rational justification. Lack of rational justification, again, is based on, for Grisez and Finnis, that God's existence is bare through natural law by "what has been made." It follows, in the Grisez-Finnis Theory, that the First Commandment is not rationally justified through the natural law.

If held consistently, this view will tend toward universalism in practical ethics, implying a lack of moral culpability for not recognizing the assumed view of the Christian highest reality. The inference Grisez and his friends attempt to make is the cosmological inference of practical reasonableness (or ICF). The goal of the NNLers is not religious conversion, per se. However, instead, it is universal recognition of the global common good (ICF), which is best explained by Christian revelation and which NNLT believes is the most reasonable worldview.

Via Negativa

Although Grisez rejects ATNLT's approach to God's existence, he nonetheless employs Aquinas's via negativa, which is to derive what God is not as a "referent" point to bring in God talk through the incommensurable good of religion. For Grisez, the argument from contingency coupled with practical reasonableness provides the most convincing argument for the existence of God, which he calls D. But D can only be known to be an uncaused entity and nothing else. Only three things can be affirmed of *D*: it is uncaused; it obtains; and it causes a contingent state of affairs to obtain.[32] Grisez states:

> *The way of negation remains. The model is suggestive; it indicates a direction that further inquiry into D might take. However, considering the model philosophically, one cannot be certain whether the inferences are sound...without some other access to D. At this point, I think, many Jews and Christians would be willing to say that D is a partial and inadequate concept of what they would call God.[33]*

The above quote confirms, for the Grisez-Finnis Theory, the inadequacy of natural revelation and natural religion by themselves, and consequently, any metaphysical and anthropological justification for God the creator through natural law. Hittinger notes that "Grisez's philosophical theology provides little positive guidance to practical reason in terms of the value of religion as grounded in a natural theology...no matter what kind of metaphysical affirmations are made about God, they would have little bearing upon practical reason anyway."[34]

In the reprint of *Beyond the New Theism* titled, *God? A Philosophical Preface to Faith*, Grisez attempts to show that the directive feature of the FPPR points to a transcendent source. "The directiveness of the first principles of practical reason is one contingent reality among others...Thus, just as the 'is' of any contingent reality points to a transcendent source of its actual being, so the 'is to be' of the principles of practical reason points to a transcendent source of their directiveness – of their prescriptivity."[35] According to Grisez, people "become dimly aware of the more-than-human source of those principles' guidance."[36]It makes people believe "they are cooperating in some way with an unseen power when they choose to act reasonably and disobeying that power when they choose to act emotionally."[37]Grisez holds that the cosmological argument and the new argument from practical philosophy together show that God is a necessary being, "incomprehensible and beyond human control. And that conclusion would provide a standard for criticizing and rejecting many of the religious worldviews that offer an alternative to monotheism."[38]In Grisez's system, it is a "referent" point for those who already believe. Hittinger perceptively identifies Grisez's goal:

> It is clear that Grisez is not attempting to demonstrate the existence of God, but is rather speaking in general of experiences which prompt interest in the good of religion. This can prove confusing because he mixes together the conclusion of his philosophical argument (that a transcendent Other exists) and general psychological (religion is attractive) and anthropological (everyone does it) observations of the sort we have encountered in his previous works.[39]

Grisez leaves room for a fideistic jump (as evidenced by the renaming of his philosophy of religion text). However, a fideism is also true for ONLT's natural religion if Aristotelian metaphysics is the basis, which Grisez explicitly rejects as sufficient to rationally justify God's existence. For Grisez, faith revealed in Christian revelation perfects the universal and incommensurable good of religion. Just as reading this paper is perfecting the incommensurable good of knowledge, so participating in the divine through faith is perfecting the universal and incommensurable good of religion that virtually all cultures have shared.

In the final chapter of *Natural Law and Natural Rights*, Finnis, too, encounters the same quandary with the via negativa since he holds to Grisez's philosophy of religion. He is unable to venture any further into NNLT's system. "Finnis's problem is that the value of religion, friendship and the common good are held in suspension (or at least, are under a "question mark") until he can find some way to verify this perspective."[40]Since Grisez and Finnis reject ONLT's metaphysical approach and acquiesce to the limitations of via negativa, the only option for the NNLers to find a solution would be to look outside the realm of ONLT's and their foundation for metaphysics. The Grisez-Finnis system continues in the same empiricist epistemology as ONLT.

The via negativa is predicated on empiricism that we must approach this alleged metaphysical absolute by knowing what it is not. However, knowing what it is not through the incommensurable good of religion does not give us any definite knowledge of this metaphysic. It is a conceding to the Kantian bifurcation of the noumenal and phenomenal. Neither the Aristotelian Unmoved Mover nor Grisez's D are sufficient for a metaphysical basis for the rational justification of natural law. Therefore, we conclude that the backdoor metaphysics of NNLT does no better in establishing a moral absolute due to its lack of rationally justifying a metaphysical absolute through natural religion and natural law.

This paper has maintained that the old and new natural law theories both rest on the assumption that they are insufficient in providing rational justification for moral responsibility. The pendulum swinging from the old natural law to the new natural law is an antinomy and does not address the significant assumption of the epistemological and metaphysical essence of the natural law. The new law's attempt to accurately represent what it believes Aquinas (and Aristotle) intended does not solve the problem of either of the natural law theories as insufficient to conclusively identify the highest reality, which is embedded in both their systems (one immediately, the other, tertiary) for the rational justification of natural law theory and practical ethics. If this presentation is sound, then NNLT is fundamentally not different than ONLT and therefore does not provide rational justification, in connection to culpability, for its morality that the natural law is clearly knowable. ONLT and NNLT must look outside their own systems to provide rational justification.

Endnotes

[1]Finnis, John. "Grounding Human Rights in Natural Law." *The American Journal of Jurisprudence*, Vol. 60, No. 2 (November 2015). 199.

[2]*Ibid.*, 148.

[3]*Ibid.*, 203.

[4]Finnis, John. *Natural Law and Natural Rights*, 2nd Ed. Oxford, UK: Oxford University Press: Clarenden Law Series, 2005. Postscript 415-416.

[5]Grisez, Germain. "The Continuity Between the Ultimate End of Human Life as Natural Reason Can Know It and the Ultimate End as Faith Teaches It to Be." *Second International Conference on Thomistic Philosophy*. Universidad Santo Tomás; Santiago, Chile; 31 July 2014. Conference Paper, 9.

[6]Grisez, Germain. "The First Principles of Practical Reason: *A Commentary on the Summa Theologiae*, 1-2, Question 94, Article 2." *Natural Law Forum Volume* 10 (1965): 168-201. Notre Dame Law School, Notre Dame, IN, 68.

[7]*Ibid.*, 168.

[8]George, Robert. *In Defense of Natural Law*. Oxford, UK: Oxford University Press: Clarendon Press Oxford, 1999, 37.

[9]Finnis, John. *Natural Law and Natural Rights*, 2nd Ed. Oxford, UK: Oxford University Press: Clarenden Law Series, 2005, 33-34.

[10]*Ibid.*, 34.

[11]*Ibid.*, 36.

[12]*Ibid.*, 36.

[13]Finnis, John. *Fundamentals of Ethics*. Washington, D.C: Georgetown University Press, 1983, 12.

[14]Stilley, Shalina. "Natural Law Theory and the "Is – "Ought" Problem: A Critique of Four Solutions" (2010). Dissertations (2009-), Paper 57. http://epublications.maquette.edu/dissertations_mu/57,

161.

[15] Grisez, Germain. "Natural Law, God, Religion, and Human Fulfillment." *The American Journal of Jurisprudence: An International Forum for Legal Philosophy* Volume 46. (2001): 3-36. Notre Dame Law School, Natural Law Institute, 33.

[16]Anderson, Owen. *The Clarity of God's Existence: The Ethics of Belief After the Enlightenment.* Wipf & Stock: 2008, 72-73.

[17]Grisez, Germain. "Natural Law, God, Religion, and Human Fulfillment." *The American Journal of Jurisprudence: An International Forum for Legal Philosophy* Volume 46. (2001): 3-36. Notre Dame Law School, Natural Law Institute, 34.

[18]*Ibid.,* 36.

[19]Finnis, "What is the Common Good and Why Does it Concern the Client's Lawyer?" *South Texas Law Review* Volume 40:41 (1999): 41-53. Scholarly Works. Paper 271. http://scholarship.law.nd.edu/law_faculty_scholarship/271, 44.

[20]Finnis, John. *Natural Law and Natural Rights,* 2nd Ed. Oxford, UK: Oxford University Press: Clarenden Law Series, 2005, 90.

[21]Hittinger, Russell. *A Critique of the New Natural Law.* Notre Dame, IN: University of Notre Dame Press, 1987, 148.

[22]Grisez, Germain, Joseph Boyle and John Finnis. "Practical Principles, Moral Truths and Ultimate Ends." *The American Journal of Jurisprudence: An International Forum for Legal Philosophy* Volume 32 (1987): 99-148. Notre Dame Law School, Natural Law Institute, 146.

[23]Staley, Kevin "New Natural Law, Old Natural Law, or the Same Natural Law." *The American Journal of Jurisprudence* Volume 38 (1993): 109-133. Notre Dame Law School, Notre Dame, IN., 128.

[24]Grisez, Germain, Joseph Boyle and John Finnis. "Practical Principles, Moral Truths and Ultimate Ends." *The American Journal of Jurisprudence: An International Forum for Legal Philosophy* Volume 32 (1987): 99-148. Notre Dame Law School, Natural Law Institute, 100.

[25]Grisez, Germain. *Beyond the New Theism.* Notre Dame, IN: University of Notre Dame Press, 1975, 12.

[26]*Ibid.*, 4.

[27]Finnis, John. *Fundamentals of Ethics*. Washington, D.C: George-town University Press, 1983, 146.

[28]George, Robert and Christopher Wolfe, eds. *Natural Law and Public Reason*. Washington, D.C.: Georgetown University Press, 2000, 56.

[29]Tollefsen, Christopher. "Natural Law and Modern Meta-Ethics: A Guided Tour," in Mark Cherry, ed. *Natural Law and the Possibility of a Global Ethics*. Dordrecht; Boston: Kluwer Academic Publishers, 2004, 40.

[30]Grisez, Germain. *Beyond the New Theism*. Notre Dame, IN: University of Notre Dame Press, 1975, 30.

[31]Grisez, Germain. *God? A Philosophical Preface to Faith*. South Bend, IN: St. Augustine's Press, 2005, XXIV.

[32]Grisez, Germain. *Beyond the New Theism*. Notre Dame, IN: University of Notre Dame Press, 1975, 230.

[33]*Ibid.*, 270-271.

[34]Hittinger, Russell. *A Critique of the New Natural Law*. Notre Dame, IN: University of Notre Dame Press, 1987, 104.

[35]Grisez, Germain. *God? A Philosophical Preface to Faith*. South Bend, IN: St. Augustine's Press, 2005, XX.

[36]*Ibid.*, XXII.

[37]*Ibid.*, XXIII.

[38]*Ibid.*, XXIII.

[39]Hittinger, Russell. *A Critique of the New Natural Law*. Notre Dame, IN: University of Notre Dame Press, 1987, 117.

[40]*Ibid.*, 153.

Étienne Gilson as Philosophical Prophet:

The Metaphysical Causes of Contemporary Terrorism, and How to Eradicate Them

Peter A. Redpath, Ph.D.

As the terrors and mass murders of the third millennium beset us daily on a global basis, prudence dictates that we seek help from people of wisdom of the past so that we might get as precise an understanding as possible of our current political situation and gain counsel from them about how we got into this trouble and sage advice about how we might best transcend it. Étienne Gilson's little known, but prophetic, opuscule, *The Terrors of the Year 2000*, written in 1948, and published by St. Michael's College of the University of Toronto, Canada, 1949, marks Gilson's reflections upon the devastations of the twentieth century and his sobering warnings about the future.[1]This is the sort of work to which people of prudence need to turn in this time of increasing international peril.

Gilson starts his reflections in this little work by noting how children of old "were taught to hold as certain that around the year One Thousand a great terror took possession of people." While scholars of his day made fun of this story, discounted it as legend, and said they could find no evidence of the "so-called panic" that was

101

"supposed to have paralyzed whole populations in the expectation of the approaching end of the world," Gilson says children of his time believed it, and "the really amazing thing" was that, as the *Chronicles* of the monk Raoul Glaber indicate, the story had some truth to it. For Glaber reports all sorts of wonders, including "a war, a pestilence, a famine, a fiery dragon and a whale the size of an island, marked the approach of the year 1000."

Approaching the year Two Thousand, Gilson contends we have witnessed far greater terrors, ones that will be a certainty for future historians even if those of the year One Thousand were not for historians of his day. Gilson then refers to the ravages of World War I, the millions of dead, his own vision of corpses of children in Ukranian villages and on the banks of the Volga; wandering "bands of children reduced to savagery, who later were to be mowed down with machine guns;" and official documentation bearing witness to the fact that "parents devoured their children. Fathers and mothers like our own, like ourselves, but who knew the meaning of that frightful word: hunger."[2]

The Communist menace overtook Holy Russia and then threatened the entire world. The bloody armistice, misnamed "peace," followed from 1918 to World War II. China remained in a continual state of war. The "barbarous civil war" followed in "Most Christian Spain."

Then came the late 1930s and the German army hurling itself upon Europe for a second time, vanquishing, plundering, butchering Poland, toppling Paris, and astonishing the world. Gilson maintains that Raoul Glaber's fiery dragons were nothing in contrast to the air bombardments that filled the skies of France, the South Sea Islands, China, Russia, Germany, Italy, and England and destroyed its once mighty navy. The atomic bombing of Hiroshima followed the genocidal holocaust against the Jews led to a contemporary age in which the close of World War II yielded no lasting peace and gave birth to the dawn of a new era "where science, formerly our hope and our joy, would be the source of greatest terror."[3]

Within a few short pages, Gilson makes clear to his reader the nature of the terror he envisions besetting the Year Two Thousand. At the close of World War II, we human beings made our most astounding discovery, whose symbolism is more striking because it is involuntary: "the great secret that science has just wrested from matter is the secret of its destruction. To know today is synonymous with to destroy."

Gilson maintains that the discovery of nuclear fission goes far beyond being an inseparable union of good and evil involving: (1) "the most intimate revelation of the nature of the physical world," (2) "the freeing of the most powerful energy that has ever been held," and (3) "the most frightful agent of destruction which man has ever had at his disposal." He maintains, "The age of atomic physics will see the birth of a new world, as different from our own age as ours is from the world before steam and electricity." This new world presents the scientist with a tragic dilemma. We know so many things today that our science might preclude our ability to control our own domination. In former times, Gilson says, we human beings mastered nature by obeying her. From now on, he claims, we master nature by destroying her.[4]

Atomic physics is only the beginning. Succeeding the era of physics, Gilson predicts we will witness "the still more redoubtable one of biology." He says that very few laboratory workers of his day doubt "we are on the verge of a great mystery which may, any day, surrender its secret. We will be able to work, not only on inert matter, but even on life, and it is not only the breadth of our power but its very nature which will become terrifying; and the more so that here again, and for the same reason, the possibility of good is inseparable from that of evil."[5]

Gilson tells us that, during his time, the "horrible" and symbolic term, "Pasteurian arms," a reference to biological warfare, has become common. Gilson finds the term more impressive because it was the exact contrary to Pasteur's intention. Pasteur cultivated microbes "to attenuate the virulence of their cultures, and thus save human lives."

He did not cultivate them, as some scientists did in Gilson's time and do today, to increase their virulence so as to kill, not cure. Given this new and destructive turn of science, Gilson predicts:

> *The biology of tomorrow will allow more subtle, but not the less formidable, interventions in human destiny. Can we imagine the repercussions which the free determinations of the sexes will have some day, perhaps in the near future? Can we picture what would happen in a world where we could not only turn out males and females at will, but select them and produce human beings adapted to various functions as do breeders with dogs or horses or cattle? In that future society which will know how to give itself slaves and even the reproducers which it needs, what will become of the liberty and dignity of the human person? For once, the most daring prophecies of H. G. Wells appear tame, for in* The Island of Dr. Moreau *they were still only working to transform wild brutes into men; in the future society, it is men whom they will be transforming into brutes—to use them to foster the ends of a humanity thenceforth unworthy of the name.[6]*

Gilson maintains that these are no idle fears. The fears of the people of Raoul Glaber's time were restricted to a small part of the Earth. Today's terrors encompass the whole planet. And the people living around the year One Thousand knew what they feared, the time of tribulation prophetically announced in the *Apocalypse*, the time when, according to St. Irenaeus, the Antichrist will devastate all the Earth, which will precede "the end of the world when creation will have lasted six thousand years."[7]

Gilson is bemused by Irenaeus's reasoning. Irenaeus, he says, "knows so many things, that the future unfolds before him with all the regulated precision of a super-film." According to Irenaeus, the world will last exactly six thousand years because one day of creation equals a thousand years. "The answer is perfect!", Gilson quips.

But, wait. What if Irenaeus and Raoul Glaber got their mathematics wrong? Suppose that the six thousand years since the dawn of creation did not come to an end around the year One Thousand. Suppose the Year Two Thousand were the more accurate date. At this point, Gilson says, "we stop smiling and an uncomfortable doubt slips into our mind." Especially so when we consider, "The scourges which have struck us, the menace of the blows which await us, do not favor abandoning this hypothesis. If the drama which we live does not announce the end of the world, it is a rather good dress rehearsal. Shall we see worse than Buchenwald, Lydice and Oradour-sur-Glane? Perhaps it is not impossible, but it is difficult to believe."[8]

At this point in his reflection, Gilson pauses anxiously, looks about, and asks, "But where is the Antichrist?" His answer, "Right there!" There he is: *Friedrich Nietzsche.*

A serious accusation. But is it justified? According to Nietzsche, yes. "*Ecce homo*, said Friedrich Nietzsche, of himself: behold the man!" (More precisely, in the section "Why I Write Such Excellent Books," Nietzsche calls himself "the *Antichrist.*" In the section, "Thoughts Out of Season," he calls himself "the first *Immoralist.*")[9] Does any man more deserve the title of Antichrist than he who brought Zarathustra's terrifying message to the modern world? Gilson thinks not. The message that Nietzsche murmurs to himself is the short sentence: "They do not know that God is dead." With Nietzsche, the transvaluation of values starts in earnest. Man wishes to make himself divine, usurp God's place, become God.

According to Gilson, Nietzsche's demonic grandeur is that he knows what he is saying and doing. He knows that God is dead. For this reason, Gilson claims, Zarathustra's "name is *Ante-christus* as well as *Anti-christus.* 'Have you understood me?' he asks. Dionysus face to face with the Crucifix." He comes "*before*" and "*against*" Christ.

Gilson considers Nietzsche's declaration "the capital discovery of modern times." Compared to Nietzsche's discovery, Gilson maintains that, no matter how far back we trace human history, we "will find no upheaval to compare with this in the extent or in the depth of its cause." Clearly, Gilson thinks that Nietzsche's declaration of God's death signals a metaphysical revolution of the highest, widest, and deepest order. Nietzsche is metaphysical dynamite. He knows it, readily admits it. "This is not just our imagination," Gilson states. All we have to do is read Nietzsche's *Ecce Homo* to find proof that what Gilson says is true:

> *I know my fate. A day will come when the remembrance of a fearful event will be fixed to my name, the remembrance of a unique crisis in the history of the earth, of the most profound clash of consciences, of a decree enacted against all that had been believed, enacted and sanctified right down to our days. I am not a man. I am dynamite.[10]*

Clearly, to Gilson, the terrors of the year Two Thousand are, in root cause, metaphysical. The chief clash of civilizations we face today is not between the politics of West and East, or the West and other political orders. It is a metaphysical clash between the ancient and modern West.

Gilson maintains that, from time immemorial, we in the West have based our cultural creed and scientific inspiration upon the conviction that gods, or a God, existed. All of our Western intellectual and cultural institutions have presupposed the existence of a God or gods. No longer. All of a sudden, God no longer exists. Worse: He never existed! The implication is clear: "We shall have to change completely our every thought, word and deed. The entire human order totters on its base."

If our entire cultural history depended upon the unswerving conviction that God exists, "the totality of the future must needs depend on the contrary certitude, that God does not exist." The metaphysical terror now becomes evident in its depths. Nietzsche's message is a metaphysical bomb more powerful than the atomic weapon dropped on Hiroshima: "Everything that was true from the beginning of the human race will suddenly become false." Moreover, mankind alone must create for itself a new self-definition, which will become human destiny, the human project.

What is that destiny, project? *To destroy*. Gilson tells us Nietzsche knows that, as long as we believe that what is dead is alive, we can never use our creative liberty. Nietzsche knows and readily admits his mission is to destroy. Hence, he says:

> *When truth opens war on the age-old falsehood, we shall witness upheavals unheard of in the history of the world, earthquakes will twist the earth, the mountains and the valleys will be displaced, and everything hitherto imaginable will be surpassed. Politics will then be completely absorbed by the war of ideas and all the combinations of powers of the old society will be shattered since they are all built on falsehood: there will be wars such as the earth will never have seen before. It is only with me that great politics begin on the globe. . .. I know the intoxicating pleasure of destroying to a degree proportionate to my power of destruction.*
> *[11]*

If Nietzsche speaks the truth about his project, which Gilson thinks he does, Gilson maintains the he is announcing the dawn of a new age in which the aim of postmodern culture, its metaphysical project, is to make war upon, to overthrow, traditional truths and values. To build our brave new world order, we have to overthrow the metaphysical foundations of Western culture. "Before stating what will be true, we will have to say that everything by which man has thus far lived, everything by which he still lives, is deception and trickery." As Nietzsche says, "He who would be a creator, both in good and evil, must first of all know how to destroy and to wreck values."

In fact, Gilson maintains, our traditional Western values are being wrecked all around us, everywhere, under our feet. He says he stopped counting "the unheard of theories thrown at us under names as various as their methods of thought, each the harbinger of a new truth which promises to create shortly, joyously busy preparing the brave new world of tomorrow by first of all annihilating the world of today."[12]

What, then, are we who oppose Nietzsche's project to do in the face of such a cataclysm? Nietzsche's plan, his mission, is to destroy "today to create tomorrow." Gilson considers forgivable that we should not have anticipated Nietzsche's advent. "But," he says, "that we should not understand what he is doing while he is doing it right under our eyes, just as we were told he would do it—that bears witness to a stranger blindness. Can it really be that the herd of human being that is led to the slaughter has eyes and yet does not see.?" Gilson's explanation for such a depth of blindness is that announcement of a catastrophe of such an order usually leaves us "but a single escape: to disbelieve it and, in order not to believe, to refuse to understand."[13]

Those who reject the escape of sticking our heads in the sand while we are sheepishly led to the slaughterhouse have another choice: to recognize the reality of the enemy we face and the nature of his project and reasonably to oppose it. Postmodern man (actually modern man on steroids) is essentially Nietzschean. And his "mad ambition" is impossible to achieve. We choose the way we can, not the way we wish. We might wish to become absolutely free creators, creators *ex nihilo*, but, at best, our wish is an impossible dream.

True creation, Gilson rightly recognizes, is not fashioning material like a demiurge. It is a totally self-authoring gratuitous act, "the only act which is truly creative because it alone is truly free." As much as we might wish to become free in this strict sense, our *esse* is always co-*esse*, not *esse subsistens*. The nature of the material world confronts us, limits us, and determines the extent to which we can fashion and remodel it. "We shall perhaps be great manufacturers," Gilson tells us. "[B]ut creators—never. To create in his turn *ex nihilo*, man must first of all reestablish everywhere the void."[14]

This, then, has become postmodern man's project: mad ambition, everywhere to reestablish the void. On all sides, postmodern man feels Nietzsche's intoxicating joy, his mad delight, in the power of destruction. When Gilson says that Nietzsche is the Antichrist, he is speaking of Nietzsche metaphorically, much like Socrates says the Delphic oracle singled him out as an exemplar of wisdom in her cryptic message to his friend Chairephon that "no one is wiser Socrates."[15] The Antichrist is postmodern man drunk:

> *With the supremely lucid madness of a creature who would annihilate the obstacle which being places in the way of his creative ambitions. Such is the profound sense of our solemn and tragic adventure. Antichrist is not among us, he is in us. It is man himself, usurping unlimited creative power and proceeding to the certain annihilation of that which is, in order to clear the way for the problematic creation of all that will be.[16]*

While Gilson does not say so specifically, the Antichrist as Gilson describes him as embodied in Nietzsche is the secularized ghost of Renaissance humanism haunting the Earth, the postmodern attempt *to supplant creation with metaphysical epic poetry effected through the unbridled free spirit of artistic destruction.* No wonder, then, that Gilson would turn to a critic of Stéphane Mallermé's poetic project to find just the right phraseology to describe "precisely the sacrilegious effort whose meaning" he sought to unravel: "to construct a poetry which would have the value of preternatural creation and which would be able to enter into rivalry with the world of created things to the point of supplanting it totally."[17]

Postmodern man's project is universal surrealism, total release of human reason, of creative free spirit, from all metaphysical, moral, and aesthetic controls; the poetic spirit, the spirit of the artist gone totally mad with the intoxicating, surrealistic power of destruction. Once we destroy everything, nothing can stop us! Since the beginning of recorded time, God has gotten in the way of the artistic human spirit, has been the "eternal obstructor" to us being total self-creators.

Now the tables are turned. With the advent of the postmodernity announced by Nietzsche, we have entered "the decisive moment of a cosmic drama."[18] Protagoras and Musaios have become Dionysus.

"Everything is possible," Gilson tells us, "provided only that this creative spark which surrealism seeks to disclose deep in our being be preceded by a devastating flame." Since "the massacre of values is necessary to create values that are really new," André Breton's description of "the most simple surrealist act" becomes perfectly intelligible and throws dramatic light upon the increasingly cavalier destruction of innocent life by terroristic acts of mass murder in our own day: "The most simple surrealist act consists in this: to go down into the streets, pistol in hand, and shoot at random for all you are worth, into the crowd."[19] (If we truly want to decrease incidences of contemporary mass murder and other acts of terrorism from the contemporary West [and the world], no one gives a better understanding of the nature of these phenomena and analysis of how to eradicate it than does Gilson.)

Since we human beings tend to be slow learners, Gilson notes that we have needed some time to grasp the full implications of the postmodern project. We have gotten out of the habit of talking about things like "divine law," but we still hold onto its vestige in our enlightened, secularized appeals to "the voice of conscience." Such appeals help us to pretend not to understand the catastrophic consequences of the grandiose sophistry of the postmodern project. If we pretend long enough that it does not exist, perhaps it will go away.

Unhappily, it will not. Gilson tells us that the father of postmodern man's existential project is Sisyphus, not Prometheus. Our destiny has become "the absurd" and "truly exhausting task" of perpetual self-invention without model, purpose, or rule. Having turned ourselves into gods, we do not know what to do with our divinity.[20]

But what will happen to us when more of us start to realize that the voice of conscience is the reflection of nothing, a convenient illusion we have created to maintain the intoxicating joy of our own poetic and sophistic project? Even drunkards, at times, tire of their alcoholism.

Gilson admonishes us that our postmodern story is really quite old. He recounts the story of Samuel from the *Book of Samuel* (8:7–22) in which the Jewish people, tired of being free, asked the aging prophet Samuel to make them a king to judge them, like all other nations had. While Samuel was saddened by their request and saw it as a rejection of him as a judge, God told him to grant the people's wish with the forewarning of the sorts of bondage that would beset them once their wish was fulfilled.[21]

Having freed ourselves from divine rule, the necessary political consequence for postmodern man is political enslavement by a totalitarian State. Having refused to serve God, we have no one left to judge the State, no arbiter between us and the State. Hence, Gilson tells us in 1948:

> *In every land and in all countries, the people wait with fear and trembling for the powerful of this world to decide their lot for them. They hesitate, uncertain among the various forms of slavery which are being prepared for them. Listening with bated breath to the sounds of those countries which fall one after the other with a crash followed by a long silence, they wonder in anguish how long will last this little liberty they still possess. The waiting is so tense that many feel a vague consent to slavery secretly germinating within themselves. With growing impatience, they await the arrival of the master who will impose on them all forms of slavery starting with the most degrading of all—that of mind. [22]*

Finding ourselves totally free to engage in the perpetual task of endless self-creation, Gilson tells us, we resemble a soldier on a twenty-four hour leave with nothing to do: totally bored in the tragic loneliness of an idle freedom we cannot productively use.[23] To Gilson's ears, the explosion of Hiroshima resounded a solemn metaphysical assertion of postmodern (better had he said "postmodern falsely-so-called") man's statement that, while we no longer want to be God's image, we can still be God's caricature. While we cannot create anything, we now possess the intoxicating power to destroy everything. As a result, feeling totally empty and alone, postmodern man (actually "modern man" on steroids) offers, to anyone willing to take it, the futile freedom he does not know how to use. "He is ready for all the dictators, leaders of these human herds who follow them as guides and who are all finally conducted by them to the same place—the abbatoir" (the slaughterhouse).[24]

So, then, now that Gilson's analysis of our "postmodern" predicament has been told, what does he offer us in the way of a solution? Precisely the sort of advice we would expect from a true and serious philosopher. He admonishes us that we will not find the remedy for our predicament by wallowing in postmodernity's evil. We will find it by courageously seeking and attacking its *metaphysical* cause. "Let us not say: it is too late, and there is nothing left to do; but let us have the courage to look for the evil and the remedy where they exist."

Since "falsely-so-called" postmodernity's chief problem is that we have lost reason (*logos* in touch with reality because we have lost God, Gilson tells us, our solution is simple. We will not find our reason and recover touch with reality again until we have "first found God again." And we will not find God again without the willingness "to receive what still remains of grace today."[25] To do that, we must turn our minds again to the world, to have them measured by the being of things, not by our unbridled and unmoored poetic imaginations.

To Gilson, this means that we must attempt once again to inhabit the universe of St. Thomas in which the service of God and reason are compatible and produce in us order, beauty, and joy—not nausea—because, in this world, unlike "the postmodern falsely-so-called," the necessary condition for the existence of one does not entail the necessary destruction of the other. For, sharing the same cause as part of the same creation, the order of our freedom, thoughts, and reality complement, they do not contradict, one another.

By submitting the measure of our minds to the being of things (which, as a practical matter, for Gilson, simultaneously entails implicit recognition of God's existence), Gilson thinks we have some hope of recovering our sanity and avoiding modernity's/postmodernity's slaughterhouse. He maintains that salvation for us today is the same as it was in Raoul Glaber's time. Glaber reported that, after all the impending anxiety, the fears of the year One Thousand subsided and peace came to the Earth. Only God can protect us from each other and ourselves. We "either serve Him in spirit and in truth," Gilson admonishes us, "or we shall enslave ourselves ceaselessly, more and more, to the monstrous idol which we have made with our own hands to our image and likeness."[26]

While what Gilson concludes in the *Terrors of the Year 2000* is true, it fails to add two things that crucially need to be said and Gilson has elsewhere maintained.

(1) As he tells us in the masterful *The Unity of Philosophical Experience*, since we are the bearers of Western culture, since it only exists in and through us and the cultural institutions we have caused, the West cannot be dying without our being aware of this reality.

By Western culture, broadly considered, Gilson says he essentially means the ancient Greek culture that the ancient Romans had inherited, which was subsequently transfused by the ancient Church Fathers with Christian religious teachings, and progressively increased by numerous artists, writers, philosophers, and scientists from the start of the Middle Ages to the present day.[27]

(2) Regarding this inherited cultural enterprise, Gilson asks a very sobering question: "Can a social order, begotten by a common faith in the value of certain principles, keep on living when all faith in these principles is lost?"

Best to illustrate the meaning of this question Gilson gives a summary description of two principles that, for him, constitute what, for brevity's sake, he calls "The Western Creed": two civilizational principles essential to the subsequent development of Western culture and all its cultural institutions.

Principle 1 is a firm belief of the ancient Greeks in the eminent dignity of human beings. As Gilson says:

> The Greeks of classical times never wavered in their conviction, that of all the things that can be found in nature, man is by far the highest, and that of all the things important for man to know, by far the most important is man. When Socrates, after unsuccessful attempts to deal with physical problems, made up his mind to dedicate himself to the exclusive study of man, he was making a momentous decision. 'Know thyself' is not only the key to Greek culture, but to the classical culture of the Western world as well. What the Greeks left to their successors was a vast body of knowledge related to man's nature and his various needs: logic, which is the science of how to think; several different philosophies, all of them culminating in ethics and politics, which are the sciences of how to live; remarkable specimens of history and political eloquence, related to the life of the city. As to what today we call positive science, the greatest achievements of the Greek genius were along the lines of mathematics, a knowledge which man draws from his own mind without submitting to the degrading tyranny of material facts; and medicine, whose proper object is to ensure the well-being of the human body. And they stopped there, checked by an obscure feeling that the rest was not worth having, at least bit at the price which the human mind would have to pay for it: its freedom from matter, its internal liberty. [28]

Principle 2 is one that Gilson was convinced had culturally saved the ancient Greeks from constructing the monstrous idol which we in the modern and Enlightenment West have made with our own hands to modern and Enlightenment man's image and likeness. Hence, Gilson identifies the second essential principle of Western culture and the

Western Creed that we had inherited from the ancient Greeks to be "the conviction that reason is the specific difference of human beings." [29] Try to transform man's specific difference from human reason and turn it into universal consciousness existing separated from the individual human body and Gilson maintains that we can no longer explain how a disembodied mind can regulate the human appetites and explain how human beings are moral agents. He states:

"Man is best described as a rational animal; deprive man of reason and what is left of man is not man, but animal. This looks like a very commonplace statement, yet Western culture is dying wherever it is forgotten: for the rational nature of man is the only foundation for a rational system of ethics. Morality is essentially normality; for a rational being to act either without reason or contrary to its dictates is to act and behave not exactly as a beast, but as a beastly man, which is worse. For it is proper that a beast should act as a beast, that is, according to its own nature; but it is totally unfitting for a man to act as a beast, because that means the total oblivion of his own nature, and hence his final destruction." [30]

Remarkable to Gilson is the centuries-long continuity within West-ern culture of these two principles inherited from the ancient Greeks by the subsequent generations. They had survived transmission to Christian culture, the Christian Middle Ages, renaissance humanism, the sixteenth-century Protestant Reformation, and even early modern discoveries in mathematical physics. So long as science remained faithful to its own philosophical, and chiefly metaphysical and moral, nature, Gilson says, "it remained the healthy exercise of reason, reason seeking to know because knowing is its natural function."[31]

Even the most stupendous progress made by the physical and biological sciences entailed no disruption in the continuity of Western culture. While man remained in control of nature (that is, retained the self-understanding of being a rational, and chiefly metaphysical and moral animal), culture could survive. It was lost from the very moment nature began to control man (that is, from the moment science became transformed into the Nietzschean will to power).[32]

Gradually, over several centuries, the dramatic material success of science re-conceived as productive and technical, mathematically-constrained knowledge essentially separated from metaphysics and ethics gradually causes Westerners:

To despise all disciplines in which such demonstrations could not be found, or to rebuild those disciplines after the pattern of the physical sciences. As a consequence, metaphysics and ethics had to be either ignored or, at least, replaced by new positive sciences; in either case, they would be eliminated.[33]

Gilson considered this move to be very dangerous, one that explains "perilous position in which Western culture has now found itself. The European burnt of his old ships before making sure that the new ones would float. Moreover, the first article of the scientific creed is the acceptance of nature as it is. Far from making up for the loss of philosophy, the discovery of scientific substitutes for it leaves man alone with nature such as it is and obliges him to surrender to natural necessity. Philosophy is the only rational knowledge by which both science and nature can be judged. By reducing philosophy to pure science (that is, the productive contemporary activity of mathematical physics), man had not only abdicated his right to judge nature and to rule it; but he has also turned himself into a particular aspect of nature, subjected like all the rest, to the necessary law which regulates its development. A world where accomplished facts are their own justification is ripe for the most reckless social adventures. Its dictators can wantonly play havoc with human institutions and human lives, for dictatorships are facts and they also are unto themselves their own justifications. "[34]

Gilson was convinced that, if we in the West lose philosophy as the ancient Greeks had conceived it, we will lose commitment to the Western Creed. In so doing, he cautioned, "we are bound to lose Western culture itself together with the feeling for the eminent dignity of man." The future of the West as he saw it was one of "an aimlessly drifting wreck, or a ship holding a steady course with a rational animal at the wheel."[35]

Clearly, Gilson thought that, in having replaced the Western Creed with the Enlightenment Scientific Creed, the contemporary West had introduced into our culture a form of psychosis which looks to irrationality as the last bulwark of liberty against a dictatorship of scientific reason and the technological system of control that it tends to generate into all our contemporary cultural institutions (like colleges and universities, political parties, religious organizations, and intellectual societies. Such being the case, and since, as Gilson tells us, (1 we are the bearers of Western culture; (2 Western culture only exists in and through us and the cultural institutions we have caused; and (3 simply as discrete individuals and disparate multitudes, we cannot recover the West dying within us, we can only do as essential psychological parts, team-members, of a culture we are aware is dying within us and our cultural institutions.

The ancient Greeks had not developed philosophy through the work of disconnected individuals, or within a short span of time. They had done so as part of a culturally-conscious, psychological enterprise, cultural team effort, to escape from the slavery they had recognized always accompanies the barbarism that human irrationality tends to generate. They had inherited their sense of philosophical wonder and conviction about the eminent dignity of the human person as a rational animal through centuries of habituation in a cultural, trans-generational psychology (or public philosophy chiefly generated out of moral and metaphysical principles transmitted through centuries of work of ancient Greek artists, poets, somewhat sound religious and political leaders, and the teachings of a Socratic public philosophy (Socratic organizational psychology) born out of, and exercised within, the Agora in Athens.

We can expect nothing different today. As Jacques Maritain, Mortimer J. Adler, and Étienne Gilson had recognized decades ago, to retrieve philosophy in our cultural institutions, we will first have to do yeoman's work of recovering it through a public philosophy within a renewed cultural psychology transmitted initially through the general population in everyday activities. Time is getting late. Please join us in this effort, with the help of grace, to turn our souls again to the world, to have them measured by the being of things, God, and a reason in touch with reality, and not by our unbridled and unmoored poetic imaginations and the despotism and terrorism it tends to generate.

Thank you.

Peter A. Redpath

CEO, Aquinas School of Leadership

Rector, Adler-Aquinas Institute

Senior Fellow, Center for the Study of The Great Ideas

02 May 2019

Endnotes

[1] Étienne Gilson, *The Terrors of the Year 2000* (Toronto: St. Michael's College, 1949), p. 5. I thank my colleague at St. John's University, Richard Ingardia, for first informing me about the existence of this work by Étienne Gilson.

[2] Gilson, *The Terrors of the Year 2000,* pp. 5–7.

[3] *Ibid.,* p. 7.

[4] *Ibid.,* pp. 7–9.

[5] *Ibid.,* p. 9.

[6] *Ibid.*, pp. 9–11.

[7] *Ibid.*, pp. 11–13.

[8] *Ibid.*, pp. 13–14.

[9]Friedrich Nietzsche, *The Philosophy of Nietzsche*, no editor or translator listed (New York: Random House, Modern Library, 1954), pp. 858, 875.

[10]*Ibid.*, pp. 14–16. While Gilson gives no specific reference to the location of this and the ones that follow passages in Nietzsche's *"Ecce Homo,* this one starts the section "Why I am a Fatality." See *"Ecce Homo,"* in *The Philosophy of Nietzsche*, pp. 923–933.

[11]*Ibid.*, pp. 16–17.

[12]*Ibid.*, pp. 17–18.

[13]*Ibid.* p. 17.

[14]*Ibid.*, pp. 18–20.

[15]Plato, *Apology*, 23B.

[16]Gilson, *The Terrors of the Year 2000*, pp. 20–21.

[17]*Ibid.*, pp. 21–22.

[18]*Ibid.*, p. 20.

[19]*Ibid.*, pp. 21–22.

[20]*Ibid.*, pp. 21–25.

[21]*Ibid.*, pp. 26–27.

[22]*Ibid.*, p. 28.

[23]*Ibid.*, p. 24.

[24]*Ibid.*, pp. 28–29.

[25]*Ibid.*, p. 29.

[26]*Ibid.*, pp. 29–31.

[27]Étienne Gilson, *The Unity of Philosophical Experience* (New York: Charles Scribner's Sons, 1963), pp. 271–272.

[28]*Ibid.*, pp. 272–273.

[29]*Ibid.*, p. 274.

[30] *Ibid.*

[31]*Ibid.*, pp. 275–276

[32]*Ibid.*, p. 276. My comments added in parentheses.

[33]*Ibid.*, p. 276.

[34]*Ibid.*, p. 277.

[35]*Ibid.*, p. 295. My addition in the parenthesis within the paragraph.

What has Athens to do with Jerusalem?

Owen Anderson, Ph.D.

I want to discuss the relationship between philosophy and theology. How are they related? Do they need to be related or do they do separate things? I'm going to look at a couple standard models and then suggest where these have come short. And I'm going to state my conclusion up front so you know what we are working toward: What these have in common is clear general revelation. And more specifically, they have in common the rejection of clear general revelation. And a little more specifically than that, they have in common the inexcusable rejection of clear general revelation so that they stand in need of redemption. And so in another way we can say that they have in common a highest goal or good: knowing God through all that by which God has made himself known.

We can sort out the common answers to this question as follows: An antagonistic relationship, a parallel relationship, and a transforming relationship. Each of these is mistaken. And we can trace this mistake to a mistaken view of knowledge and the good.

Take for instance the view that says these are in tension. This view says something like there is natural knowledge and there is revealed knowledge. And natural knowledge leads us to something like Plato or Aristotle at best, more likely something like Epicurus. None of these get us to the God of the Bible. So the knowledge of God that is given in the Bible must come in and replace this other natural knowledge. The God of scripture replaces the God of the philosophers and idolaters.

Or consider the view that says they are parallel. This view says that they are doing different kinds of things. A person can affirm truths in philosophy and affirm contradictory truths in theology because they are in different realms. This could be softened by saying philosophy is literal and theology is poetic. Or it could be affirm that they about the same thing and in the same sense and it is ok for them to contradict (Averroes).

Then there is the view that says these are related in a transformative way. This says that the natural philosopher does the best he can and then theology is added to get him the rest of the way. Theology transforms philosophy to get it to where it needed to be. The theologian might use some of the tools of philosophy, some of the theistic arguments, and then add the God of the Bible and the redemptive message of Christ.

You can begin to see where each of these takes a piece that is important. For instance, one might emphasize that all men are created in the image of God and so get some things right. Perhaps it is a focus on the fact that there are different fields of human study that have different methods. Or another might emphasize the reality of total depravity and that apart from regeneration no one can know God. But behind each of these is the presupposition that there is a God and that there is sin and that there is a need for redemption.

The idea that purported special revelation somehow solves problems for humans in Athens, or puts them back on the right course, or offers a parallel field of study, is what needs to be shown and not merely asserted. This gets us right into how a person understands knowledge. That a person or books makes a claim does not make the claim true. A prophet or his writing needs to be tested. Nor does the claim being true translate into it being understood. Humans can accept special revelation in a fideistic and legalist fashion without understanding or benefit just like humans can reject special revelation without understanding or benefit. And so these traditional solutions reveals to us a failure going into the problem. It is a failure Jerusalem shares with Athens, a failure that theologians share with philosophers. It is a failure of meaning.

And noticing that is what leads us to the answer we will pursue here. Rather than begin with assumptions about philosophy and about theology we find that what both Athens and Jerusalem have in common is thinking. And more specifically, thinking about the highest good.

So what do we mean with thinking? And why start there? We start there because it is self-evident that we think. This is self-evident because to deny it we would be doing it. You might think you recognize this from Descartes who began with "I think therefore I am." But Augustine said the same thing much earlier. And Plato begins with distinguishing opinions and knowledge.

We can also say that it is self-evident that there are laws of thought. Again, consider the opposite. When we think we are making distinctions between things. Like 'a' and 'non-a.' This includes distinguishing thought from non-thought. That gives us the laws of thought. Identity, non-contradiction, and excluded middle. A is A, it isn't non-A, and something is either A or non-A. These cannot be doubted because they make doubt possible. If the "a" is confusing insert any terms. God is God. By reason we can recognize God and distinguish God from non-God.

These laws of thought are what we call reason. This is different than reasoning, or naturalistic thinking (often the root of Athens v Jerusalem division), or rationalizations. By reason we form concepts, judgments, and arguments which are the forms of all thought. If we tried to think of another form we'd be using one of these. When we put together an argument we are doing just this. And it is here that we see the use of reason. We use reason to form thoughts, and we use reason to critically analyze thoughts. We use reason to interpret our experiences and ask what they mean. And we use reason to build coherent systems and world views.

We can distinguish thinking from sensations, impressions, feelings, intuitions, and related terms. A thought makes an assertion by combining or disconnecting concepts. For example, God is real. We can analyze this in two ways: what does it mean and is it true or false. We have to take them in that order. A meaningless sound is neither true nor false. What is meant by "God?" This is an ambiguous word and so we cannot yet say if it is true or false that God is real.

So what do Athens and Jerusalem have in common? Thinking. Or, the use of reason to find meaning. We've defined thought and reason. What is meaning? We can think of meaning in a couple of ways. One of them is purpose. When we ask what is the meaning of something we are asking what is its purpose. This connects up to what is the nature of the thing. The good for a being is according to the nature of that being and from that we gets its purpose. We are familiar with the question: what is this for, what does it do? And we can apply this to our life: what is the purpose of human life what is it for?

But there is another sense of meaning more basic than this sense. This is cognitive meaning. We can distinguish this from practical meaning and psychological meaning. Practical meaning is not only what was discussed above about purpose. It tends to be a non-cognitive functionality. Psychological meaning is rooted in the feelings and has to do with a sense of well-being. But when we begin to give these cognitive expression we have left them are now thinking. This is aimed at cognitive meaning. Meaning is present when the laws of thought are used, and when the laws of thought are violated then meaning is lost. For example, to say that "a is non-a." This has the form of a belief, connecting two concepts together, but it does so in a way that violated the laws of thought. It doesn't mean anything. Common examples are a square-circle and being from non-being.

We want meaning in this sense and it relates directly to our purpose. It is human nature to want to understand. When we don't understand we feel the meaninglessness and boredom that come with it. It is unbearable and we will go to extreme ends to avoid meaninglessness.

Can we have meaning? Our thinking is ordered. Thinking is not random. It is not a scattered collection of thoughts. It is ordered presuppositionally. This means that there are basic things and then there are less basic things that build on these. If we cannot have meaning at the basic level then we will not have meaning at any level that presupposes this. It might appear that we agree and have meaning at a less basic level. For instance, we might all agree that we are at this talk. But this agreement quickly disappears when we ask what we each mean by this. This simple questions brings out the very point of presuppositional thinking and meaning. What is it to be a human? What is it to be in a room? Are we materialists? Spiritual monists? Dualists? Theists? Each of these mean different things by this apparently simple statement and the agreement disappears because we did not agree at the more basic level.

Can we have meaning? Yes, if we think presuppositionally. If we identify our most basic beliefs and test them for meaning. This is a logical structure but it also comes out in a dialogical structure. The logical structure flows from beliefs about value, to beliefs about what is real, to beliefs about how we know. And the dialogue will follow this same pattern. A person will make a claim about what is good, and follow-up questions require that person identifying what they believe is real, and then they are pressed on how they know this.

There is something else both Athens and Jerusalem have in common. On the one hand it is thinking. But in another sense it is not thinking. Or, not seeking. No one seeks. So while we will see formal similarities between thinkers we find that they are ultimately all in this condition. By "formal simliarity" is meant that all thinkers use reason to forms concepts, judgments, and arguments. All thinkers have concepts about authority, being, and the good. This is true in Athens and in Jerusalem.

Even so it is also true that no one seeks. How can we combine these? We see both that humans have a rational nature and that humans deny this rational nature. We see both that humans need meaning and that humans have rejected the use of reason to find meaning at the basic level. This means that although it is clear to reason that God the Creator exists, humans have replaced God with almost anything imaginable. Humans have said of the creation that it is eternal—without beginning. Humans have called non-God "God". They have sought ends but not what is actually the highest end. It is from this condition of not seeking that humans, both in Jerusalem and Athens, need redemption.

I am focusing on "not seeking" but it is worth noting that this progresses into not understanding and not doing what is right. We may have a tendency to focus on the "not doing what is right" part especially as we complain about injustices others have done. But this is a product of the earlier problems of not understanding and not seeking. This condition is sometimes likened to death, or is itself properly what is the real death with physical death standing in relation to this.

So to describe what Athens and Jerusalem have in common in this negative sense is that the same spiritual death of not seeking, not understanding, and not doing what is right. This means that they are in the same need of what has been called regeneration. And notice how this need for regeneration addresses the problem of what they have in common. They are in the condition of not seeking and need to begin seeking. This is not something added to either that is extra. Nor is it parallel. Neither can they said to be in tension since both need that same thing.

Instead, to clearly state what Athens has to do with Jerusalem, it is: they share in common that it is clear to reason that God exists and both can know this from general revelation. They also share in common that neither seek, neither understand, and neither do what is right and therefore they are in need of regeneration. This is a restoring to the life of seeking. It is what all can know about God from the works of God. These works include the work of creation but also redemption. All humans need this redemption, the regeneration just spoken about, and how God accomplishes it is itself another instance of revelation about God. All of this points to the knowledge of the glory of God through God's works of creation and providence.

I want to give a concrete example of this. And in a way it answers the problem of Athens and Jerusalem. What do these have in common? Let me say "Babylon." And why Babylon? This could be taken historically to recall the story of Babel and the original unity of humanity. A unity in unbelief. It is after this unity is divided that we start the story of redemption in Abraham. It might also call to mind the current reality that humanity is reunited in a way not seen since that time. Under what law are they now united?

But we can also take Babylon as a type. It is representative of humans not seeing what is clear. Abraham had to leave Babylon. He argued against their use of idols. These are arguments he could have gotten from general revelation. The sun and moon are not eternal and were created. The creator should be worshiped not the creation. So Babylon serves as a type not just of universal humanity but universal humanity in: not seeking to know what is clear; because of this in attributing the eternal power of God to some aspect of the creation; and in doing this to putting the self in the place of God in determining good and evil.

I think we can especially see this come out as humans wrestle with the existential problems of life, the problem of evil. So let us look at the Babylonian Job, or Babylonian theodicy. It is an obvious comparison to the Biblical Job. We can use both examples to illustrate the point made above.

The Babylonian Job asks a very relatable question. How can the life of happiness, of bliss, be assured or attained? Not only doesn't he know, he is also under what he considers to be unfair suffering. Let's read:

> *Sufferer VII*
> *33~Can a life of bliss be assured? I wish I knew how!*
> *67~Your mind is a north wind, a pleasant breeze for the peoples.*
> *68~Choice friend, your advice is fine.*
> *69~Just one word would I put before you.*
> *70~Those who neglect the god go the way of prosperity,*

71~While those who pray to the goddess are impoverished and dispossessed.
72~In my youth I sought the will of my god;
73~With prostration and prayer I followed my goddess.
74~But I was bearing a profitless corvée as a yoke.

Here we have a standard expression of the problem of evil: the good seem to suffer and the wicked do not. And yet we also have an unreflective idolatry. It is nice how it comes out here because many might be in the same kind of idolatry and not know it. This person has neglected the clear general revelation of God and exchanged the eternal power of God for idols.

Friend VIII
78~My reliable fellow, holder of knowledge, your thoughts are perverse.
79~You have forsaken right and blaspheme against your god's designs.
80~In your mind you have an urge to disregard the divine ordinances.
Sufferer
135~I will ignore my god's regulations and trample on his rites.
Friend
219~Follow in the way of the god, observe his rites,

Like Job, the Babylonian Job also has friends. And we see that the friend charges him with having turned from the god. And the Babylonian Job doesn't disagree. Unlike Job who argues for his innocence, the Babylonian Job affirms that he will ignore the god's rites.

Sufferer
244~The god does not impede the way of a devil.
251~How have I profited that I have bowed down to my god?

Friend
255~In your anguish you blaspheme the god.
264~Though a man may observe what the will of the god is, the masses do not know
   it.

Here again the sufferer complains that the evil prosper and that having bowed down to the god has done no good. We see this complaint in the wisdom literature although here the sufferer does not come to a satisfactory answer. It is worth nothing that the friend states that the masses do not know the will of the god. If the masses do not know the will of the god they cannot keep the will of the god.

Friend XXVI
   276~Narru, king of the gods, who created mankind,
   277~And majestic Zulummar, who dug out their clay,
   278~And mistress Mami, the queen who fashioned them,
   279~Gave perverse speech to the human race.
   280~With lies, and not truth, they endowed them for ever.
   281~Solemnly they speak in favour of a rich man,
   282~"He is a king," they say, "riches go at his side."
   283~But they harm a poor man like a thief,
   284~They lavish slander upon him and plot his murder,
   285~Making him suffer every evil like a criminal, because he has no protection.
   286~Terrifyingly they bring him to his end, and extinguish him like a flame.

By way of contrast again with Job's friends, here the friend recounts the Babylonian creation narrative. Humans are created evil or perverse (and not very good). This is an attempt at solving the problem of evil. Humans are wicked and that is why they suffer. They inflict suffering on each other. And they do this because that is how the gods created them. For the Babylonian polytheist there is not a "problem of evil" like there is for the theist. In theism, God is perfect in goodness and power and so we ask "why is there evil?" God could have created a world without evil, and God would want to have created a world without evil. But for the Babylonian there is not a similar problem with respect to their gods. However, this also means that there is no room for the original complaint by the sufferer. We see that in the end the sufferer simply returns to hoping the god/goddess will show mercy.

> *Sufferer*
> *287~You are kind, my friend; behold my grief.*
> *288~Help me; look on my distress; know it.*
> *289~I, though humble, wise, and a suppliant,*
> *290~Have not seen help and succour for one moment.*
> *291~I have trodden the square of my city unobtrusively,*
> *292~My voice was not raised, my speech was kept low.*
> *293~I did not raise my head, but looked at the ground,*
> *294~I did not worship even as a slave in the company of my associates.*
> *295~May the god who has thrown me off give help,*
> *296~May the goddess who has [abandoned me] show mercy,*
> *297~For the shepherd Šamaš guides the peoples like a god.*

We see here that he reaffirms himself as having done what is right. He views himself as wise. It is the gods who have thrown him off. Perhaps if he continues his worship they will give him mercy. The gods are changeable and rule based on their mood. One of the problems for the sufferer is that he has not been able to answer his question or really any question. Why is there suffering? How can a life of bliss be assured? The gods are temporal and changeable, is anything eternal and unchngable? It seems that knowledge is not possible and so meaning is not possible. We can contrast this with Job.

Job 28:28 (Job)
> *And to man He said,*
> *'Behold, the fear of the Lord, that is* wisdom,
> *And to depart from evil is* understanding.

We find Job affirming the central piece of Biblical Wisdom Literature. It is a stark contrast with the Sufferer. There is wisdom, there is understanding, and these are related to knowing God and the difference between good and evil. *Fear* here involves realization of the rule of God; God is real and rules in our lives. There are consequences for our actions. Sin leads to death. Departing from evil is understanding and brings life.

Job 32:26-28 (Elihu

> *Then that person can pray to God and find favor with him, they will see God's face and shout for joy; he will restore them to full well-being. And they will go to others and say, 'I have sinned, I have perverted what is right, but I did not get what I deserved. God has delivered me from going down to the pit, and I shall live to enjoy the light of life.'*

What is absent in the Babylonian account is both the eternal un-changable God and the reality of human sin. Elihu introduces the reality of sin, the need for repentance, and that humans have not gotten what they deserve because of God's mercy. Contrast this with the Sufferer who believes he has been wrong and has no hope but that perhaps the gods will change their mind.

Job 35:9-13 (Elihu)

> *People cry out under a load of oppression; they plead for relief from the arm of the powerful. But no one says, 'Where is God my*

Maker, who gives songs in the night, who teaches us more than the beasts of the earth and makes us wiser than the birds in the sky?' He does not answer when people cry out because of the arrogance of the wicked.

Elihu continues this theme: no one turns to God. We saw the sufferer turn to his idols, but no one turns to God the creator. No one seeks God. Suffering plays the role of a call back from this condition. The Sufferer did not hear this. Will Job? Job's friends had accused him of secondary sins of which he was innocent. None of them got back to this root level of sin.

Job 36:24-26 (Elihu)
"Remember to extol his work, which people have praised in song. All humanity has seen it; mortals gaze on it from afar. How great is God—beyond our understanding!"

Elihu concludes that the works of God are a source of the knowledge of God available to all. God is incomprehensible or beyond our understanding in the sense inexchaustible. This returns our minds to the theme of the fear of the Lord. The Babylonian gods may have been terrible in their petulant use of their power but God is infinite and perfect and this should result in humble worship of God. When God addresses Job we see that all of the content is about general revelation. Has Job seen what is clear about God from the things that are made?

Job 38:1-5 and 38 (God)
Then the Lord answered Job out of the whirlwind, and said:
"Who is this who darkens counsel
By words without knowledge?
Now prepare yourself like a man;
I will question you, and you shall answer Me.

"Where were you when I laid the foundations of the earth?
Tell Me, if you have understanding.
Who determined its measurements?
Surely you know!
—-
Who has put wisdom in the mind?
Or who has given understanding to the heart?

All of this discourse emphasized the difference between God and the creation (non-God). This is a clear distinction known by reason. All of general revelation demonstrates this. God is the infinite, eternal, unchagable creator and man is not. All of what man has invented to put in the place of God are empty idols. This is a deeper level of sin than Job's friends got to. There was sin in Job (he was blameless, not sinless) and it had to do with the root sin committed by all humans. When God shows this to Job we see this response:

Job 42: 1-6
Then Job answered the Lord and said:
"I know that You can do everything,
And that no purpose of Yours can be withheld from
You.
You asked, 'Who isthis who hides counsel without knowledge?'
Therefore I have uttered what I did not understand,
Things too wonderful for me, which I did not know.
Listen, please, and let me speak;
You said, 'I will question you, and you shall answer Me.'
"I have heard of You by the hearing of the ear,
But now my eye sees You.

Therefore I abhor myself,
And repent in dust and ashes."

This repentance distinguishes Job from the Sufferer. Job comes to know God in a deeper way. His repentance includes a hatred of the sin of noting having known God as he should have. And this is a universal condition of not seeking and not understanding. Job repents at that deep level and not merely the superficial level suggested by his friends.

I am relying on Job as an example that makes use of general revelation truths even though the book itself is in special revelation. Job is blameless but not sinless. His friends try to accuse him of fruit sins and on this they are wrong. In a similar way the Babylonian Job denies having done this kind of sin. He claims he is wise and pious. Elihu and then God speak to Job. God points to what the creation reveals about Himself. This is content that Job could have and should have known. He had access to these same truths about creation. In his response we see the difference between these Jobs. Job hears these truths from God as conflicting and he repents. His friends are told to offer a sacrifice for their sins. After Job does this with them and prays for them he is restored two-fold.

What do we see then is the relation between Athens and Jerusalem? I'm saying Babylon. Why? Because of what we see in the Babylonian Job. Here is a human, trying to understand, feeling the strain of the call back from natural evil and the pressure of it all seeming meaningless. He never considers his own need for repentance of idolatry. He has neglected the general revelation of God. He should repent. Job repents of this when confronted with his sin.

In Athens we have this problem. In Jerusalem we have this problem. And so I said that what these have in common is general revelation. They have in common their human nature as thinkers who want meaning. But they also have in common the rejection of clear general revelation. They have in common the need for redemption. This need is revealed in general revelation although how it is achieved is a matter for special revelation.

The philosopher should know what is clear about God. The theologian should do this as well. Theology does not begin in revealed religion or special revelation. It begins in natural theology. Natural theology is the study of general revelation and so here we see theology and philosophy overlap. The models above did not capture this. Truth cannot be contradictory, or in tension/conflict with itself, and the transformative view failed to capture the clarity of general revelation.

Permit me one final example. In my book *Faith and Reason at Early Princeton* I contrast the condition of American education now with the condition of the Academy at the time of Cicero. Just like the Academy under Plato had begun with the goal of knowledge of the good, so too the American Academy coming out of the First Great Awakening at Princeton had started with the goal of the knowledge of God and piety. By the time of Cicero the Academy was physically in ruins repressing its intellectual ruin in Academic Skepticism. Today, the American Academy is in the same Academic Skepticism. It is the rejection of knowledge (no knowledge is possible and embracing the consequences including not understanding good and evil.

In a discussion with Cicero, Cato says the following about Jupiter: Like the Babylonian Sufferer, Cato puts an idol in the place of the eternal Creator. Like the Babylonian Sufferer, Cato can make no sense of suffering and at his best only has piety to his idol as a final resort. Babylon, Athens, Rome, and Jerusalem all have in common the ability to know God from general revelation. They also have in common their own not seeking, not understanding, and not doing what is right. When Job was presented with this in his life he repented and came to know God in a deeper way.

One last caution or word of warning. It has been the case that philosophers and theologians sometimes unite on the highest good. I mentioned this idea in the beginning. They may try to unite in a false good the way that we found in the story of Babel mentioned a moment ago. A common example of this for philosophers and theologians is the beatific vision. This phrase can have many meanings but what I mean here is a direct, non-cognitive vision of God in the afterlife. Plato and Aristotle are taken to advocate for this. And theists are found to do the same. It stands in direct contrast to what Job found as his highest good. Specifically, the knowledge of God through the works of God. This knowledge of God is cognitive and mediate (known by the works of God, not directly).

Even when we find Plato and Aristotle advocating for this we find the kind of philosophical ambiguity that highlights our need to think presuppositionally. The theists do not mean the same thing by "God" as the Greek dualists. So any apparent unity about the beatific vision quickly disappears upon examination.

A non-cognitive vision sets aside human nature, thinking, knowledge, and meaning. We have question, as we found with the Babylonian Job, and a non-cognitive vision does not answer these. It is a neglect of the works of God (taking the Lord's name in vain). So we need to avoid this false unity by turning to the example given by Job. The works of God are the source of the knowledge of God and we have neglected this. Which Job will be our model?

The Good as Resistance

Kelly Fitzsimmons Burton, Ph. D.

My good friend, Owen Anderson, in his book *The Natural Moral Law: The Good After Modernity*[1], argues for the need for a natural moral law based upon the Good as the source of unity for humankind in the context of a "new global reality." In this book, he cites the U2 song "The Wanderer," written for Johnny Cash, in which Cash sings about the citizens who say they want the kingdom, but they don't want God in it. What this pop-culture reference alludes to, and what Anderson gets to in his book, is the reality of a "kingdom." Similar to St. Augustine, I want to contrast what I will call "the kingdom of God" with the "kingdom of man," to show how the Good is a source of unity for human life in "the new global reality" of which Anderson speaks. I want to use the analogy of "kingdom" as a form of polis that unites mankind in the "new global reality." A kingdom is a way of thinking about the global unity of humanity under a unifying principle.

My paper is about the Good as a source of unity and resistance to contemporary collectivism on the one hand and individualism on the other hand. My method is an act of retrieval philosophy. This means I am going to the past to address philosophical questions of the present. I will be retrieving concepts of classical philosophy. My goal is to challenge our thinking about the current political scene and mere political acts of resistance. I would like to show that there are philosophical assumptions that we are not addressing that give rise to the dominance of politics. This paper is inspired by ongoing conversations with my mentor, Surrendra Gangadean, whose original contribution to Ethics I hope to build upon in this paper, and Catholic philosopher Peter Redpath, who challenges us to see philosophy as the attempt to understand the one and the many, unity and diversity. Dr. Redpath also personally challenged me to go on the offensive in doing philosophy. This is my attempt.

The original context of delivering this paper was the Spring 2019 Ethics section of the American Academy of Religion West Coast conference, where the central theme was: *Religion and Resistance.* Ethics is one branch of philosophy. So my paper is in the area of the philosophy of religion. Philosophy is essentially the human soul's quest for the *logos*, so I argue in my recent work.[2] Eva Brann says that Western Philosophy begins with the dual concepts of *logos* and *ontos*.[3] Reason and being. The *logos* is the word, reason, account, form, *ratio*, genus. It is Aristotle's formal cause. The *logos* is in humans as reason (our form), and it is in the world as rational principles that may be known by us (forms, laws, *ratio*). Philosophy's quest has been to explain the source of this *logos* – rationality – in us and in the world. That the world is knowable to us creates in us a sense of wonder. Philosophy begins with wonder. We wonder at the nature of things and try to name the things we discover.

Dr. Redpath says:

> *During the high points of ancient Greek culture and the high middle ages of Christendom, metaphysics was viewed as "first philosophy." It was recognized to be the only discipline that existed capable of judging the nature, divisions, and methods of the different arts and sciences, the only human science that could rationally judge the other sciences and rationally explain how they relate to each other and justify their existence in relationship to human life as a whole.*[4]

In another place Redpath says:

> *In its generic definition,* philosophy is chiefly a cooperative-and-transgenerational, individual and cultural, psychological enterprise (or organizational psychological habit) *essentially devoted to contributing to our individual and cultural understanding of how to solve "The Problem of the One and the Many: how many individual things essentially become parts of one, composite, organizational whole and essentially act the way they do."*[5]

I want to look at this part/whole relationship that Redpath points us toward in terms of the *logos*, the good, and a kingdom.

The early Greek philosophers had a difficult time grounding the *logos* in being. They assumed materialism and could not explain why or how matter should be ordered - supremely ordered - and rational. The early Christians, particularly the Apostle John, had an explanation for the source of the *logos*. God, the second person of the Trinity, is the *Logos* – the Word - through whom all things were made. John's Prologue describes the word in man as the light by which he understands. The *logos* is in the world as created by God – in natural law - by which man was to know God. The Psalms are replete with statements such as "the heavens declare the glory of God." The created order is a revelation of the existence and nature of God. John also talks about the rejection of the *logos* and the grace of God in coming to his own through prophets bringing the word/*logos* of redemption. That too has been rejected, so the *Logos* – the Word – comes incarnate to redeem humankind from the sin of rejecting the *logos* in himself, in the creation, and finally in the scriptures.

So far, my story has been that of the Greek and the Christian search for the *logos*. This story and all that goes with it became the foundation for Western Civilization. Somewhere in our history the foundation cracked and is now crumbling.

I would like to present a hypothesis about where things went wrong, and how to re-orient ourselves for the future. I want to begin with the present. We no longer talk about philosophy as the Greeks, and early Christians did – as the search for the *logos*. Instead, philosophy has assumed a position of skepticism and a practice of pragmatism. We have many theories, but none of them can claim Truth. We have to get on with the business of living, so power, or politics, become the dominant force in our public life. Emotions run high, lawsuits abound, and we are all afraid of the fury of the mob. Where is the voice of reason? Philosophy should be the voice of reason.

We should return to the search for the *logos*. This is a paper about ethics. Is there a *logos* - an organizational principle – for ethics? A genus, as Redpath would say? Aristotle seems to think so. Yet, he may have been less clear than he could have been in giving us guidance in this area. What he does give us are the main concepts of ethics — the good, virtue, and happiness. The good is the *logos* of ethics. It is the organizing principle for our values, choices, and action. It guides the virtues as means to achieving the good and happiness as the effect of possessing the good. The good for a being is based on the *logos* – the nature of – a being.

The good for human beings is based on human nature. Aristotle says humans are rational political animals. Plato thought that humans had a soul that was rational, emotional, and volitional. We have lost that concept of a soul today. Christianity affirms that a human is a body-soul unity. The body-soul unity is what makes humans distinct from angels and animals. That we are political means, we cannot escape the reality of human community - the *polis*. Our rationality is fundamental to and is to rule over our animal nature and to organize our political life together. In this sense, human beings are fundamentally rational.

The good for human beings is based on our rational nature. It is good for humans to use reason to understand the nature of reality, all aspects of reality, and reality as a whole. It is harmful to humans when they do not use reason to understand the nature of reality. When we fail to understand, we fail to choose and to act appropriately. The good is the end in itself, the goal of all goals, the *summum bonum*. As such it is the organizing principle for human life both individually and collectively and historically. The good is the source of unity for human beings. It is our *logos* for life. Philosophy should help us to discover the good and to choose wisely for the good.

In the Christian tradition, this end in itself is found in the words of Jesus "now this is eternal life that they might know you and Jesus Christ whom you have sent." Eternal Life is a quality of life that abounds through knowing God. It starts in this life, and it extends for the rest of eternity. The good for human beings is knowing God. Historically, this comes out in the Westminster Shorter Catechism question one: what is man's chief end? Answer: Man's chief end is to glorify God and enjoy him forever. Philosopher and natural theologian, Surrendra Gangadean, pulls these ideas together from the Westminster standards and summarizes this way: "man's chief end is to glorify God through all that whereby he maketh himself known, in all his works of creation and Providence" until the earth is full of the knowledge of the glory of God.

The goal of knowing God takes us back to the theme of the *logos* – the good for man is to know God through what God has revealed of himself in the created order (the *logos* in the world) and in Providence (redemptive rule in human history). How is man to know God? We know God through the original work of mankind, which is also our philosophical work, by naming things. We know God by understanding the nature of things – the *logos* in the world reveals the *logos* who created the world. We are called to rule, to have dominion. What is it to rule? What is dominion? These are philosophical questions. What *is* it? What does it mean?

Rule and dominion require work - intellectual work, understanding our own powers and the nature of things, and physical work, expending energy to develop the powers in the world. In the historic Christian tradition, this is called the cultural mandate. We are to go from the Garden of Eden to the City of God – the kingdom of God.

After the fall, we have more work to do. We have to rule over sin in ourselves, in our families, in the church, in the state, and in the world. There is no need for the state pre-fall. That should tell us a bit about the nature – *logos* – of the state. It exists to restrain evil by means of the physical sword.

With God's grace in the story of redemption for the world comes the mission mandate: "go and make disciples of all the nations teaching them to obey all that I have commanded." This does not do away with the cultural mandate. All the nations of the world were to come into the kingdom of God on the earth. The Lord's prayer says: "Thy kingdom come, thy will be done, on earth as it is in Heaven." How do we imagine this kingdom? What is its nature? Can philosophy and the search for the *logos* help us here?

Philosophy helps us to look at whole/part relationships as in the one in the many. What are the parts of a kingdom (a whole)? We can start with citizens. Citizens are people with diverse personalities, backgrounds, and talents who are born into a family, the first institution of any *polis* or kingdom. An institution is a unifying principle (Redpath's genus) that must have a goal. If we get the goal wrong, then disunity will result. What is the nature and purpose of a family? How is family related to the good? What is the purpose of children? Can ethics help us to answer these questions?

We live together as political beings, and under a fallen condition, with real evil in the world, so the kingdom must have a government. What is the nature and purpose of government? What are its form (*logos*) and function? What should be the basis of the legal code in a government system? What should be the relationship between governments? Should ethics be able to help us in this area?

We need to be taught to rule over our sinful nature; we need spiritual discipline. This is the nature and purpose of the church. The church is for discipleship of its members and worship of God. The church bears the sword of the spirit - the Word of God. Can ethics give guidance in the nature, purpose, and role of the church in the kingdom? Does the church have a genus?

How do we gain an understanding of reality, human nature and its capacities, the virtues and human excellence past and present? How do we gain an understanding of the physical world and its potential? This is the nature and purpose of education. Including the humanities and the arts, and the sciences and technology. What is the nature and goal of education? Can philosophy help us to answer this question?

Education (as well as family, church, and *polis*) has a role in developing all humans and each unique human with their unique talent given by God for the good. Talent is how we achieve the good. Talent is how we exercise dominion and rule. It is how we create value and wealth. When we create value, and exchange what is of value, we have the need for an economic system. *Oiko nomos* is the law for the household; it begins as household management. It is the *logos* for the home. In the context of the kingdom of God, we must manage the resources of the whole earth. What is the wise use and management of our resources? Philosophy, as the love of wisdom, should be able to guide economics. Is there a best economic system for the good? What about capitalism? What about communism?

Both capitalism and communism assume that human beings own absolutely. The reality is that nobody owns anything absolutely, especially in a world where God creates. We all die, and we cannot take a thing with us. We are given talent for the purpose of the good. God gives talent equally and differently, but we do not develop our talent equally. This is where economic disparity comes in. Social justice should involve providing equal access to the development of talent for the good. We are managers, stewards, over what we have for a time and for the purpose of the good. The good should direct us in what we value. It should guide us in how we gain, use, and accumulate capital. The good should give us an economic ethic that respects the talent of the individual, the contribution of the community to the development of that talent, and the inheritance we leave to future generations who will also need the good and contribute to the good. Ethics should be able to speak to us about value, talent, economic justice, and about wise applications in the institution of the economy.

If we pay attention to the nature (*logos*) of these institutions and the goal of the good (the *logos* of life) we should be able to rule with wisdom in each aspect of life now and into the future (everlasting life). Philosophy as the search for the *logos* informs us about the nature and goal of each thing that is. Philosophy helps us to identify and name the diverse aspects of reality and to understand the order and relations of reality. In addition, philosophy informs us about human nature, the goal of life, and the virtues and vices. Philosophy helps us to identify the institutions of the polis and the means of preserving and advancing the human project – building the kingdom of God.

What happens when philosophy ceases as the search for the *logos*? What happens when philosophers decide that there are no natures in things? When they decide human beings are not essentially rational but are essentially animal, driven by desire and not by reason? What happens when philosophers conclude that all is matter and that there is no God? When this happens, as has happened, we end up with the kingdom of man on the earth. The kingdom of man is what we see now when we look out on the political scene. It is the *polis*, soon to become the "new global reality" without God as Creator of natures/*logos* and determiner of good and evil for beings. In the city of man, because there is no *logos* to speak of and because man is not essentially a rational being, desire must be obtained and maintained by means of power.

The modern and postmodern philosophers may deny the *logos* in the world (a real genus), but they cannot avoid the *logos* of philosophy itself, which is systematic in so far as it is involved in undergirding worldviews, which are whole part relationship/organizations. The kingdom of man has all the same organizational structures and formal philosophical assumptions that support those structures as the kingdom of God, it's just that the content of those assumptions is different. The kingdom of man denies that the world itself is rational (ordered by *logos*). It assumes that all is matter. It assumes that human beings are material beings driven primarily by desire. Consider Rousseau, Darwin, Marx, Freud, and Nietzsche as examples of proponents of the kingdom of man.

If the satisfaction of desire fundamentally motivates humans, then the good for this kingdom is happiness or comfort or pleasure. Imagine all the institutions of culture organized for the goal of pleasure. What is the family for? What is religion for? What is government for? What is education for? What is the economy for? What is the purpose of human effort and work? All are for the satisfaction of our desires. The organizational principle of all of culture is for the satisfaction of desire? Will that ultimately satisfy human beings? Or do we need more?

Here is where our contemporary political scene comes into play again. The kingdom of man is divided into the left and the right. Both seem to agree that the goal of life is the satisfaction of desire or pleasure. But what should take priority, the collective satisfaction of desire (what in Ethics is called utilitarianism), or the individual satisfaction of desire (egoism and/or hedonism)? Without the voice of reason, how do we decide this? Without reason, power decides. The state becomes the dominant sphere of the polis for the kingdom of man.

Let us consider each. On the left, there is a move towards a political collective where the state owns absolutely. And the state determines the nature of the other institutions of the polis such as the family, economics, religion, education. The goal seems to be the maximization of happiness for the greatest number of people. This is why the political is seen as all-encompassing and why everything is economics on the left. It is consistent with Marxism and the view that what determines a persons standing is primarily class. Today we have changed class to race and gender and possibly even sexual identity. The highest virtue of this version of the kingdom of man is equality. We all need equal distribution of the means of happiness. Happiness requires income, so we need equality in terms of the distribution of income. Question: where are the virtues to check human vice in this view of the kingdom of man? I am thinking especially of the vice of sloth. Is a lifetime of work for the collective satisfaction of desire worth it? Why put forth the effort? Can satisfaction of desire be the goal of life?

On the right, there is a move towards self-rule where individual autonomy is prized above all else, and the highest value is freedom: freedom to pursue happiness (satisfaction of desire). However, how does this work with the institutions of the polis where an individual pursues their own satisfaction of desire to the exclusion of the collective? Does the individual determine the goal and purpose of the family? What is the purpose of the economy for the individual? Is it to maximize income so as to maximize happiness? What about the church? Is the purpose of the church determined by the individual? Is this why we see the dominance of individualism (and emotionalism) in religion today? What about the state? Does the individual pursuit of happiness lean towards libertarianism and the minimization of state regulation? This view tends to promote the privatization of everything. Does the individual own absolutely? Here is the problem for individualism: where are the virtues to check human vice, especially greed? Again, can satisfaction of desire be the chief end?

From a classical philosophical perspective, the contemporary swings to collectivism on the left and individualism on the right are mistakes. These mistakes stem from having the wrong goal. The wrong goal comes from a mistaken view of human nature, ultimate reality, and finally the failure to search for the *logos*. It is a failure of contemporary philosophy, which has left off the search for the *logos* and has, in fact, become anti-*logos*. Neither the state directing the collective nor the autonomous self-direction of the individual is wise enough to know the good and the means to the good in every choice of life in every institution of culture. This is why we need to do philosophy, and this is why we need to do ethics. It is also why we need the cumulative insight of the past. We need a retrieval of the good - the *logos* of life. The Good serves as resistance to contemporary political divisions and is a source of unity for all of human life and activity. As an act of resistance to the kingdom of man, we need to retrieve the kingdom of God and the goal of that kingdom. But first, philosophy must return to the search for the *logos*.

Endnotes

[1]Anderson, Owen. *The Natural Moral Law: The Good After Modernity* (Cambridge: Cambridge University Press; 2012).

[2]Burton, Kelly Fitzsimmons. *Retrieving Knowledge: A Socratic Response to Skepticism* (Phoenix:Public Philosophy Press; 2018).

[3]Brann, Eva T.H. *The Logos of Heraclitus: The First Philosopher of the West on Its Most Interesting Term* (Philadelphia: Paul Dry Books; 2011).

[4]Redpath, Peter. *A Not-So-Elementary Christian Metaphysics*, Volume 1 (St. Louis: Enroute Books; 2015), p10.

[5]Redpath, Peter. "An American Perspective on the Christian Philosophy of St. Thomas Aquinas: Midwife to Birth of a New and Improved Global Civilization of Freedom." Paper delivered at the Cardinal Wyszynski University, Poland, June 2018.

Blaise Pascal's Apologetic Program:

On The Insufficiency of Reason and the Defense of Fideism

Arturo Gastelum

Introduction

Rene Descartes and Blaise Pascal stand as the two chief French representatives of two conflicting traditions: rationalism and fideism.[1]Descartes embarked on the quest to discover a philosophy adequate for the Christian worldview, where he deliberately attempted to be "the first of all men to overthrow the doubts of skepticism.".[2]He relied on the use of reason through his *Methode naturalle* to arrive at indubitable truths upon which the whole edifice of human knowledge could be erected.[3]Descartes, like Pascal, challenged skepticism by carrying it to its logical conclusion, yet Descartes did not end up in fideism but instead, in rationalism for he believed that when philosophy—properly and diligently applied—does not unsettle human certainty, but strengthens it.[4]

Pascal, on the other hand, pursued the path of fideism in large measure as a reaction to the perceived excesses of Descartes' rationalism.[5]According to Pascal, Descartes' philosophical approach leads to a deistic God, whose only function lies in "setting the world in motion; beyond this he [Descartes] has no further need of God."[6] Descartes' God is the God of the philosophers, while Pascal worshiped the God of Abraham, Isaac, and Jacob.[7] Pascal labored fervently to undermine the rationalist claims to knowledge. He attempted to establish the superiority of faith over reason by questioning the sufficiency of reason to attain knowledge of the self, God, the human condition, and the need for redemption. *Pensees* (thoughts is Pascal's apologetic treatise where he lays out his objections to rationalism and develops his case for fideism. It has been deemed the primary source for understandig Pascal's method and its erudition has earned the right for high esteem as "one of the most remarkable apologetic works ever penned."[8]

The significance of his work is heightened by his contribution to fideistic apologetics, as well as his engagement with the prominent intellectual challenges of the Reformation, the revival of Greek skepticism, and Descartes' rationalism.[9] In *Pensees*, upon close ex-amination, lies latent a formidable critique of reason. Although not systematically stated—yet through careful analysis—one can uncover Pascal's comprehensive attempt at refuting the role of reason in philosophy, religion, and apologetics. My aim in this work is to gain a greater understanding of Pascal's foundational contributions to the discourse of faith and reason in apologetics; to identify specific arguments advanced in his work, and to begin formulating a future response to safeguard the place of reason in apologetics.

The approach to this paper is fourfold: (1) to identify the specific arguments dispersed throughout *Pensees* that are used to undermine reason as a source of knowledge in philosophy, religion, and apologet-ics; (2 to elucidate the arguments given by Pascal to justify fideism and the primacy of revealed religion over and against natural theology; (3) to succinctly respond to the arguments against reason; (4) and lastly, to respond to the arguments given for fideism and revealed religion.

Pascal's Apologetic Project: Undermining Rationality to Establish Fideism and Revealed Religion

Pascal's apologetic method, although lacking systematic arrangement in Pascal's writings, has nonetheless been outlined and explained.[10] The difficulty consists in attempting to locate the specific apologetic school of thought wherein his system belongs.[11] Irrespective of the discussion regarding apologetic schools, his aim is clearly discernible: Pascal sets out to humble man by exposing the woeful limitations and challenges that reason faces in its attempt to establish itself as the basis of epistemic certainty. The humbling of man extends beyond reason's failure to grasp the meaning of reality; for Pascal divorces man from God's handy work by declaring the creation an inconclusive expression of the being of God, rendering the world epistemically ambiguous.

In Pascal's view, we do not possess enough evidence from our perception of the world to either affirm or deny the existence and nature of God—by implication, Pascal rejects the possibility of natural theology. We—as humans—find ourselves in a paradoxical limbo where we are forced to make a decision for or against God, but neither reason nor reality are able to justify our choice. We are compelled by the wretchedness of our fallen state and the longing for happiness to find an answer elsewhere. Pascal proposes faith as the answer, along with inherent knowledge—*sensus divinitatus*—imprinted in the human heart, and the special revelation provided in the Bible by God himself concerning his will and purpose for mankind.

Faith and reliance upon the Scriptures are the answer to our dilemma. Therefore, according to Pascal, we ought to set aside the obstacles that hinder our embracing of the gift of revelation. Cast reason aside for it is but a defective tool; do not seek after natural theology for it leads to weak proofs deserving of contempt; humble yourself by abandoning autonomous pride and forsake the love of the flesh which enslave us

150

to its cravings; and lastly, our succor lies in listening to God—who has gifted to us in grace access to His truth, and in his mercy has condescended to make his truth known in the incarnation and the Scriptures. Faith in God and knowledge through Scripture suffices to find life everlasting. We cannot help but choose—the wager is presented to all. Would we gamble what is of infinite value to preserve what is perishable? Pascal leaves the reader with the responsibility to choose wisely.

Arguments Contra Reason

In *Pensees*, Pascal details a series of arguments aiming to conclusively prove the insufficiency of reason to attain knowledge in philosophy, religion, and apologetics. His arguments attempt a cumulative case against reason where reason in its three forms—*in itself, in its use, and in us*—come short of knowledge, and in fact he compels us to recognize the need to go beyond reason and embrace salvation through faith. The cumulative case elaborated by Pascal argues against reason *in itself* by claiming that it is impotent to attain knowledge, that reason's inherent result is the awareness of human misery, and that reason when consistently applied leads to skepticism (intellectual despair.

Reason in *its use* fails at several levels: it is incapable of grasping the incomprehensible relation that exists between the finite and the infinite; it is inadequate for solving the problem of arriving and justifying first principles in philosophy; it lacks the precision to settle disputes in ethics; and ultimately it is a menace to the necessity and existence of revealed religion since it renders it superfluous.[12]

In us, reason raises awareness of our wretched fallen condition, yet it lacks the ability to provide lasting meaning for our existence. Thus, reason helps us see the misery of our natural state and the utter hopelessness of our existence apart from revealed religion and may perhaps be useful to understand and defend revelation, but ultimately it is of no help to discern foundational truths. This series of objections, according to Pascal, in the end, compels us to heed the path of true understanding provided to us by God in the Scriptures of the Old and New Testaments. In the following section the arguments against reason—stated above—will be exposited to enable us to see the compelling case that Pascal attempts to make.

According to Pascal, reason is impotent to answer basic questions in philosophy, fruitless in apologetics, and blind to its own limits. In philosophy, the fundamental question of origin (*arche* and purpose of things (teleology are beyond our grasp for they "are hopelessly hidden from him [man] in an impenetrable secret; he [man] is equally incapable of seeing the Nothing from which he was made, and the Infinite in which he is swallowed up."[13] The largeness of the conceptual objects (origin and purpose leave man in the dark. Moreover, reason is faced with the problem of understanding substances (matter and spirit and the body-soul duality. Both transcend our cognitive abilities; "What completes our incapacity of knowing things is the fact that. . . , we are composed of two opposite natures, different in kind, soul and body."[14] The body-soul duality makes our condition all the more unintelligible in spite of its counter intuitiveness:

> Who would not think, seeing us compose all things of mind and body, but that this mixture would be quite intelligible to us? Yet it is the very thing we least understand. Man is to himself the most wonderful object in nature; for he cannot conceive what the body is, still less what the mind is, and least of all how a body should be united to a mind.[15]

Pascal extends his attack beyond metaphysics (origin, purpose, and dualism) to the central concept in ethics—'the good'.[16] After a long history in the quest to understand the good as grounded in human nature, no agreement has been secured, "One [philosopher] says that the sovereign good consist in virtue, another in pleasure, another in the knowledge of nature, another in truth, another in total ignorance, and another in wondering at nothing."[17]Lack of agreement on the definition of the good, according to Pascal, must imply its unknowability by reason. So far in the history of ideas, the use of reason in philosophy "has gained us nothing certain."[18]

Pascal makes his assessment all the more clear in a disdainful remark evaluating the entirety of philosophy and its history, for if the conclusions of philosophy were true, "we do not think all philosophy is worth one hour of pain." In apologetics, the role of reason is fruitless—it terminates in futility. The traditional proofs (ontological, cosmological, and ontological arguments) are contemptible since they do not conclusively prove the existence and nature of God. Soteriologically, reason is incapable of bringing a person to believe because the conversion of the unbeliever is done apart from reason and argument, it is the sole work of the Holy Spirit. Conversion is a supernatural act administered by God through the Holy Spirit; therefore, reason has no say in it. Traditionally, apologetics via natural theology has prominently used the design argument—proving the existence of a divinity from the works of nature.

According to Pascal, inferential proofs from the creation are very weak proofs. In fact, instead of being a compelling argument, "I [Pascal] see by reason and experience that nothing is more calculated to arouse their [unbelievers] contempt."[20]Proofs and arguments in apologetics fall short of persuasion, they lead only to obscurity and darkness: "For those in whom this light [the living faith] is extinguished, and in whom we purpose to rekindle it, persons destitute of faith and grace, who, seeking with their light whatever they see in nature that can bring them to this knowledge, find only obscurity and darkness."[21]The act of believing depends on the sovereign act of God who in His mercy inclines some to believe, led to faith by their hearts without recourse to their intellects or proofs.[22]The necessity for reason in apologetics is nullified in Pascal's approach; he dismisses the effectiveness of the design argument to persuade unbelievers by making God the only cause of regeneration. Thus, rendering reason inadequate, more precisely, futile and therefore useless to convert through argumentation.

In addition to rejecting the use of reason in philosophy and apologetics, Pascal proceeds to explicate that reason itself is 'not reasonable.' Reasonableness entails knowing one's limits and proceeding no further. On the contrary, rather than abandoning its quest for truth in the face of abysmal failure, reason remains dogmatically determined to attain knowledge. Pascal explains that, "She [reason] is reasonable enough to admit that she has been unable to find anything durable, but she does not yet despair of reaching it; she is ardent as ever in this search, and is confident she has within her the necessary powers for this conquest."[23]

Pascal's depiction of reason resembles the futile quest of the knight errant Don Quixote for it neither has an object nor the means to fulfill it. Furthermore, neither Don Quixote nor reason are their own masters; the former is guided by incongruent unattainable ideals and the latter is subservient to the passions—"All our reasoning reduces itself to yielding to feelings," and when our feelings clash, and we feel the need for resolution, reason does not succeed as arbiter because "it is pliable in every sense" by the feelings.[24] Pascal portrays reason as engulfed in a feat of hubris or madness: unable to recognize its own limitations, while lacking self-determination, presses on in its futility—without attainable goals or enduring accomplishments.

The misfortunes of reason exceed its impotence to attain knowledge in philosophy or apologetics. Pascal clearly outlines the inherent consequences that follow from the use of reason: it inevitably leads to ever deeper degrees of skepticism (intellectual despair), and it increasingly raises awareness of our miserable human condition. Both realities—skepticism and misery—serve a redemptive purpose in Pascal's project: they lead to seeing the need for Scripture to rescue us from the uncertainty of reason and the hopelessness of skepticism. Skepticism is instrumental because it "neutralizes man's rational impulses,"[25]and awareness of human misery compel us to seek lasting happiness in God.[26]

First, we will address the human condition. Pascal provides several statements describing the depth and misery of mankind apart from God— "life under the sun."[27]He makes use of common experience, history, and biblical accounts to corroborate his assessment. The wretchedness of man lies at several levels. In some descriptions Pascal emphasizes the wickedness of the human heart: "Man is, then, only disguise, falsehood, and hypocrisy, both in himself and in regard to others. He does not wish anyone to tell him the truth; he avoids telling it to others, and all these dispositions, so removed from justice and reason, have a natural root in his heart."[28]In other descriptions Pascal accentuates man's inability to properly diagnose his condition: "What a chimera, then, is man! What a novelty! What a monster, what chaos, what a contradiction, what a prodigy! Judge of all things, imbecile worm of the earth; depository of truth, a sink of uncertainty and error; the pride and refuse of the universe!"[29]and also, "Man does not know in what rank to place himself. He has plainly gone astray and fallen from his true place without being able to find it again. He seeks it anxiously and unsuccessfully everywhere in impenetrable darkness."[30]

Yet in other descriptions Pascal takes special care to highlight how lost man is: "When I see the blindness and wretchedness of man, when I regard the whole silent universe and man without light, left to himself and, as it were, lost in this corner of the universe, without knowing who has put him there, what he has come to do, what will become of him at death, and incapable of all knowledge, I become terrified."[31]At the basis of Pascal's description of the human condition is man's inability to know the nature of the self, the world, and God. Skepticism underlies the misery of mankind. If man's reason would adequately yield true knowledge of the world, then hope would lie in its use. Instead, Pascal believes that the use of reason itself will inevitably result in the terrified perplexed state of intellectual despair, where we develop a fuller awareness our misery. After exploring Pascal's view with regard to the relation between reason and the self; we will proceed to examine Pascal's arguments to undermine reason's ability to understand the world.

Pascal's objections against reason itself—as the laws of thought—begin at the most foundational level. Pascal's central objection is not about the laws of thought themselves, but against their ability to produce new knowledge. In a proposition such as: "God is, or He is not. To which side shall we incline? Reason can decide nothing here."[32] The law of noncontradiction enables us to logically distinguish and diagram propositions, but it does not, and cannot dictate which proposition is true. Here Pascal believes that reason ought to fall prostrate to the insurmountable existential and philosophical problems that reality presents to us—the truth of the world eludes the grasp of reason.

Pascal seeks to strengthen the veracity of his skepticism about reason by pointing at the abysmal history of philosophy—the great philosophers that have preceded us did not produce proofs that have withstood the test of time, and neither has a consensus been attained in philosophy. By implication, if they who were great and who sought to use reason to the fullest failed in their attempts, then pitiful is our situation for attempting to seek further than nature has endowed us the ability to attain:

> It is in vain, O men, that you seek within yourselves the remedy of your ills. All your light can only reach the knowledge that not in yourselves will you find truth or good. The philosophers have promised you that, and you have been unable to do it. They neither know what is your true good, nor what is your true state. How can they have given remedies for your ills, when they did not even know them?[33]

The collective failure of mankind to settle the perennial questions that have preoccupied men from its beginnings are themselves a great source of discouragement, and an occasion to fall prey to skepticism. Yet, that is not the only worrisome development from 'the philosophers,' for they have been responsible for inflicting great damage to ethics and religion. In ethics, philosophers have been guilty of disregarding basic questions such as the immortality of the soul: "It is certain that the mortality or immortality of the soul must make an entire difference to morality. And yet philosophers have constructed their ethics independently of this: they discuss to pass an hour."[34] Pascal reproaches the philosophers for neglecting to address a central question in ethics that serves as a necessary precondition for ethics—the immortality of the soul. If this question is not settled, then ethics cannot be discussed. To engage in discussion without first addressing it is tantamount to no more than "to discuss to pass an hour." Thus, in Pascal's view ethics has suffered under the rule of the philosophers and their pretense of knowledge.

Furthermore, Pascal charges the philosophers/logicians for desecrating what is holy. "It seems that their license must be without any limits or barriers, since they have broken through so many that are so just and sacred."[35] The failure of philosophy transcends philosophy itself; it affects adjacent disciplines like theology. Reason has claimed a magisterial role to judge the truth of Scripture; it has questioned doctrines such as original sin, imputation, the incarnation, and has invalidated miracles contained in the Scriptures.[36] Pascal responds to the intemperate claims of reason by calling the rationalists to regulate their pretensions since their problem is primarily moral and not philosophical; what is needed is modesty and humility on their part. They must recognize that those who love God—whatever kind of intellect they may have, high or low—are those who have a humble heart, and who love lowliness.[37] Part of developing humility originates in properly understanding the frailty, unreliability, and limits of the intellect. For Pascal something as common as forgetting a thought that we entertained and wanted to commit to writing should serve as an occasion to properly reassess the power of the intellect: "In writing down my thought, it sometimes escapes me; but this makes me remember my weakness, that I constantly forget. This is as instructive to me as my forgetting thought; for I strive only to know my nothingness."[38]

The theme pursued by Pascal of tempering the claims of reason—to function as a magistrate of truth—are further substantiated by addressing 'inherent' limitations in the use of reason. Particularly, he deals with two basic problems in philosophy: (1) the relation between the finite and the infinite; (2) reason's ability to arrive at and justify first principles. Both problems have plagued philosophy from its inception, and both problems if successfully established would shift reason's role from magisterial (the judge of revelation) to ministerial (handmaid to revelation). It is the latter that Pascal understands as the proper role of reason in the life of the believer: "It is not by the proud exertions of our reason, but by the simple submissions of reason, that we can truly know ourselves."[39]

Pascal raises several objections about reason's inability to understand the relation of the finite and the infinite. At the level of attitude, Pascal charges "the attempt to arrive at the knowledge of the whole, is a presumption as infinite as the object of knowledge." Pursuit of the knowledge of the infinite entails an infinite presumption—an expression of epistemic hubris.[40] Ontologically, for the finite to pursue knowledge of the infinite requires a logical impossibility—it entails that the finite becomes the infinite or shares "in an infinite like nature."[41] The logical impossibility resides in postulating that the finite (created and limited) can become like the infinite (uncreated and unlimited). In addition, Pascal highlights the epistemological problem of comprehending anything at all since knowledge of the parts cannot be attained apart from knowledge of the whole and knowledge of the whole cannot be attained without knowledge of the parts: "How can a part know the whole? But he may perhaps aspire to know at least the parts to which he bears some proportion. But the parts of the world are so related and linked to one another [by causation, dependency, mediacy] that I believe it impossible to know one without the other and without the whole."[42]

Pascal further objects to our ability to know God emphasizing the disparity that exists between the finite and the infinite. He conceives of these two concepts equivocally (vs. univocally or analogically) since there is no point of connection or relation between the two kinds of being or existence: "If there is a God, He is infinitely incomprehensible, since, having neither parts nor limits, He has no affinity to us. We are then incapable of knowing either what He is or if He is. This being so, who will dare to undertake the decision of the question? Not we [humans], we have no affinity to Him."[43]

Pascal pursues his aim of 'humbling' reason still yet further. He questions the profitability of seeking and attaining knowledge itself by pointing to its hollowness in two senses. On the one hand, increased knowledge compared with infinitude amounts to nothing— "What matters if that man should have a little more knowledge of the universe? If he has it, he but gets a little higher. Is he not infinitely removed from the end, and is not the duration of our life equally removed from eternity?"[44] On the other hand, the being of God as infinite so overwhelms our finite existence that it annihilates it in its presence, including our conceptions and knowledge: "The finite is annihilated in the presence of the infinite, and becomes a pure nothing."[45] Consequently, after delineating the limitations that haunt reason in its attempt to breach the gap between the finite and the infinite, Pascal exhorts us to apply reason to the task that it can in fact perform: "The last proceeding of reason is to recognise that there is an infinity of things which are beyond it. It is but feeble if it does not see so far as to know this."[46]

The second basic problem in philosophy used by Pascal to expose the frailty of reason to attain knowledge lies in the quest for "first principles" or "principles of philosophy." He acknowledges that our natural condition and inclination longs to find such principles, and that all philosophers have stumbled in seeking an answer: "We burn with desire to find solid ground and a firm foundation whereon to build a tower reaching to the infinite. But our whole groundwork cracks and the earth opens to abysses."[47] The answer Pascal proposes requires recognizing that reason has no part in the grounding or understanding of first principles. "It is by the heart that we know first principles; and reason which has no part in it, tries in vain to impugn them."[48] The role of reason consists in "trusting the intuition that proceed from the heart, and must base them in every argument."[49] In the end, Pascal proposes an alternative source of authority and knowledge which rests not in reason but in innate intuitions existing in the human heart. Those intuitions stand beyond the domain and reach of reason. They are necessary presuppositions that reason must assume and not seek to examine; for "principles are intuited," while "propositions are inferred."[50]. Inferential knowledge belongs to the domain of philosophy, intuition resides in the human heart—unarrived by axioms or deductions.

Additionally, to the objective and inherent limitations of reason, Pascal brings to light the subjective difficulties that arise when reason acts in combination with sense datum and the passions—reason's reliability is further diminished:

> *Man is only a subject full of error, natural and ineffaceable, without grace. Nothing shows him the truth. Everything deceives him. These two sources of truth, reason and the senses, besides being both wanting in sincerity, deceive each other in turn. The senses mislead Reason with false appearances, and receive from Reason in turn the same trickery which they apply to her; Reason has her revenge. The passions of the soul trouble the senses, and make false impressions upon them. They rival each other in falsehood and deception.*[51]

The portrayal of the human person and its epistemic sources leave men destitute from any reliable claims to knowledge. To heighten the attack on our ability to properly ascertain reality, Pascal brings a relevant example that will later be more fully articulated by David Hume. The example concerns our belief in the reliability of the laws of nature based on observation; it is a grave attack for it calls into question causality itself and the knowability of natural laws: "When we see the same effect always recur, we infer a natural necessity in it, as that there will be a tomorrow, etc. But nature often deceives us, and does not subject herself to her own rules."[52]

Effectively, Pascal has launched a full-scale attack undermining any grounding for reason to claim knowledge of reality. His objective consisted in leading reason to recognize its total and incurable skepticism. After arriving at that recognition, Pascal has compelled the rationalist to seek out a different source of knowledge—one that according to Pascal, provides an unshakable foundation. Pascal believes that by presupposing the existence of a good God, he has solved the problem that hindered the rationalist from achieving their objective. The reasoning goes as follows: "The reliability of any knowledge depended on the reliability of our faculties. And the reliability of our faculties depended on their source. If they have been created by a good God, then we can rely on them."[53]Although arguably a circular argument, Pascal sees it as necessary and sufficient to accomplish the end of accounting for the reliability of our epistemic faculties.

Thus far, Pascal's work consists in negative apologetics—for he has engaged in identifying the limitations and inadequacy of reason to attain knowledge but has not yet provided a positive response to the questions. If he were to stop at negative apologetics, his contribution would have been critical (assessing the validity of reason) but not constructive (developing a system to answer the questions in philosophy, religion, and apologetics). Instead, Pascal proceeds to layout a positive apologetics that provides arguments for the primacy of faith and revealed religion to attain certainty and knowledge. In Pascal's apologetical program, faith and revelation safeguard Christianity's most important elements (mystery and the supernatural), while the primacy of reason accomplished the opposite aim for it would undermine its mysterious and supernatural elements by rendering them irrational—making reason antithetical to Christianity since in Pascal's view, Christianity is primarily a supernatural religion made true precisely because of its mysterious character.

Pascal's Positive Apologetics: Arguments for Faith and Revealed Religion

Although Pascal began his apologetics by raising skeptical challenges to reason, his intent is not to defend skepticism and its implications, but to overcome it. Pascal is more accurately characterized as a fideist than a skeptic; even though it should be noted that both skepticism and fideism share a common assumption—denying the knowability of basic things through reason. Since there are many forms of fideism, we must first proceed by defining and clarifying the kind of fideism supported by Pascal. In general, "fideists are persons who are sceptics with regard to the possibility of our attaining knowledge by rational means, without possessing some basic truths known by faith."[54] Pascal's form of fideism—while denying reason the foundational role of testing and justifying basic presuppositions—does not altogether reject the use of reason: "[fideism] denies to reason any complete and absolute certitude of the truth prior to the acceptance of some proposition or propositions by faith, even though reason may play some relative or probable role in the search for, or explanation of, the truth."[55] Stated in Pascal's own words, "If we submit everything to reason [rationalism], our religion would have no mysterious or supernatural element. If we offend the principles of reason [absolute fideism], our religion would be absurd and ridiculous."[56] The role of reason begins after the foundational beliefs contained in the heart are embraced by faith.

The functions of reason within Pascal's framework are two: reason is used to understand the meaning of divine revelation; and reason is used to expose the incoherence of opposing worldviews by evaluating the soundness of their beliefs. What reason is not permitted to do is to assess the veracity of the intuitions of the heart—this is the ministerial use of reason. The intuitions of the heart possess their own rationale which exclude and transcend reason: "The heart has its reasons, which reason does not know."[57]

Pascal's apologetic program argues for the necessity of special revelation in light of the alleged failure of reason to secure knowledge; it is by special revelation, according to Pascal, that knowledge and meaning is accessible to us. In Pascal's assessment, apart from revelation, we are trapped in nihilistic skepticism where the existential burden would be unbearable: "without the Scripture, which has Jesus Christ alone for its object, we know nothing, and see only darkness and confusion in the nature of God and in our own natures."[58] Our ignorance in the absence of Scripture can only be remedied through Scripture, "through Jesus Christ, and in Jesus Christ, we prove God, and teach morality and doctrine."[59] It is by Scripture that the succor of men is found, otherwise, "Without this divine knowledge [Scripture] what could men do but either become elated by the inner feeling [pride] of their past greatness which still remains to them, or become despondent [despair] at the sight of their present weakness?"[60] Both extremes—pride and despair—can and should be avoided by embracing the truth provided through divine revelation. In fact, revelation provides more than an antidote against pride and despair, it provides the answer to soteriological concerns regarding the need for, and attainment of salvation.

Divine revelation confronts us with knowledge of both our wretchedness (fallen humanity) and the attainment of eternal life (the knowledge of God). In Pascal's view both are needed and they require proper context to avoid despair or hubris, "since it is equally dangerous to man to know God without knowing his own wretchedness, and to know his own wretchedness without knowing God."[61]Knowledge of God without conviction of sin and death leads to the God of deism; while knowledge of sin and death without God leads to an existential crisis. Only special revelation avoids both lamentable extremes.

In Pascal's view we are trapped in a paradox whose only solution lies in dogmatic fideism. Pascal describes our state as one of "open war among men, in which each must take a part and side either with dogmatism or scepticism."[62]We find ourselves in a "tangle" where "Nature confutes the sceptics, and reason confutes the dogmatists," and "we cannot avoid one of these sects, nor adhere to one of them."[63]Then the solution lies in embracing revelation as the final answer that may free us from our paradoxical state: "Humble yourself weak reason; be silent, foolish nature; learn that man infinitely transcends man, and learn from your master your true condition, of which you are ignorant. Hear God."[64]It is through revelation that we become delivered from our wretchedness and come into the light of truth. The Christian faith is that truth for it accounts for "The corruption of our nature, and redemption by Jesus Christ."[65]The Scriptures become the source and foundation of knowledge that accurately provides insight about our fallen nature, our need for salvation, the atoning work of Christ, and in addition proves its own veracity through "morality, doctrine, miracles, prophecies, and types."[66]

The only legitimate form of theology for Pascal is revealed theology. Natural theology does not figure prominently within Pascal's system for it requires that reason be able to understand the revelation in the creation, and that there be an objective clear revelation to be uncovered in creation. Both conditions are denied by Pascal. He conceptualizes the world as epistemically ambiguous:

I see on all sides and I see darkness everywhere. Nature presents me nothing which is not matter of doubt and concern. . . Wherefore I have a hundred times wished that if a God maintains nature, she should testify to Him unequivocally, and that, if the signs she gives are deceptive, she should suppress them altogether; and that she would say everything or nothing, that I may see which cause I ought to follow.[67]

In addition to the ambiguity of nature, Pascal adds the 'hiddenness of God' or *"Deus absconditus"*[68] for He "has left men in darkness."[69] Yet, that attainment of knowledge through natural theology is not altogether denied; since Pascal admits that the knowledge of God through the creation is possible for "some souls to whom God has given light, yet is false [not possible] with respect to the majority of men."[70]

But even for those who can discern the footprint of God in the creation, their argument from design are very weak proofs that arise contempt. The last and most famous attempt by Pascal to "incite the search after God"[72] is the "wager argument." Given our inability to know the world through reason, the epistemic ambiguity of the world, and the hiddenness of God, "we have no option but to wager. We are embarked. Which will you choose then?"[73] Pascal encourage us to make a willful decision for "happiness" and to minimize the role of reason in deliberation: "when one is forced to play, he must renounce reason to preserve his life, rather than risk it for infinite gain, as likely to happen as the loss of nothingness."[74] Since we are thinking beings, and since by nature we make and cannot help but choose, then choose for lasting happiness: "If you gain, you gain it all; if you lose, you lose nothing."[75] This, Pascal believes to be an ethically justified decision that can be argued for conclusively: "If men are capable of any truths, this is one [the wager for the infinite]." And if we are to wait until certainty is attained before we act, then we ought not act in religion for it is not certain. Furthermore, if we are not to act until we attain certainty, we must do nothing at all for certainty is not possible.[76]Pascal's wager argument compels us to make a decision of incomparable value; for it is a decision that culminates with the promise of everlasting life and happiness—which is the ultimate end of human action.

Response to Arguments against Reason

When we wish to correct with advantage and to show another that he errs, we must notice from what side he views the matter, for of that side it is usually true, and admit that truth to him, but reveal to him the side on which it is false.[77]

The arguments presented by Pascal and explained above are numerous and comprehensive in nature. In response, an attempt will be made to concisely address basic uncritically held assumptions that Pascal used to corroborate his objections to reason, while acknowledging legitimate insights that motivated Pascal's attempt to provide an alternative apologetic program. Pascal himself has strived to give credit to the perspective of his opponents, and simultaneously seeking to correct their errors, I will endeavor to emulate him.

It is noticeable that while Pascal devotes a significant portion of his writing to pointing out perceived shortcomings in the use of reason, little attention is given to defining reason itself. The closest Pascal comes to an attempt concerns the distinction between the mathematical and intuitive minds. The former operates systematically by inference from basic postulates or axioms to specific conclusions, while the latter operates non-systematically and non-inferentially, it takes hold of basic principles all at once. Those principles are felt and not deduced. The two kinds of minds are barely intelligible, if not utterly unintelligible to one another for the intuitive mind's

BLAISE PASCAL'S APOLOGETIC PROGRAM:

intuitions are "felt rather than seen" and making them felt by those that do not perceive them entails the greatest difficulties; while "men of intuition who are purely intuitive cannot have the patience to reach to first principles of things speculative and conceptual."[78] It is unclear whether the basic distinction between the two kinds of men described is one of habit or nature. If the intuitive man had developed patience by exercising his mind in mathematical thinking, would he be able to make those principles known to the mathematical man who fails to intuitively perceive them? Or is the exercise of the mathematical minds itself alienating and destructive of the intuitive principles?

Elsewhere in *Pensee*, Pascal speaks of intuitions as residing and proceeding from the heart, which gives the impression that they are universal in that those intuitions are inherent in human nature. If so, what is their content and how does one account for objectively having them yet subjectively not acknowledging their existence? Moreover, are the intuitions cognitive in nature? Do they involve concepts, judgements, and arguments? Or does Pascal prescribe that there exists a form of thought beyond or besides concepts, judgements, and arguments? If the principles of the heart exist, and they are so numerous,[79] as claimed by Pascal, what are they? Or is Pascal willing to postulate a form of knowledge that transcends the known categories of thought and ventures into non-cognitivism; where knowledge evades concept formation and where what can be known cannot be grasped or expressed in discursive logic? If the latter, then Pascal's claim to intuitive knowledge may be an appeal to an unknown, and as such, would do little to settle disputes regarding philosophy, religion or apologetics.

Pascal justified the rejection of philosophy and the philosophers in light of the known abysmal failure of philosophy for over 2,000 years to arrive at definitive positive agreement. Here, Pascal is justified in noting the deplorable state in which philosophy finds itself. But it is one thing to acknowledge the failure to arrive at the desirable outcome, yet another to despair on the possibility of ever arriving. Progress has taken place in philosophy; it has not been a total failure for "to agree that we have not come up with a satisfactory answer is a significant agreement. We agree on what does not work, even if we have not come up with a satisfactory answer."[80] The failure of philosophers to use reason to arrive at satisfactory answers does not itself become an indictment of either philosophy or reason, but it may perhaps be more appropriate to lay the blame in the 'doers' of philosophy rather than philosophy itself, as well as blaming the 'users' of reason rather than reason itself.

Pascal's rejection of the traditional proofs—ontological, cosmological, and teleological arguments—has been all the more justified since he denounced them as weak and contemptible. The Enlightenment has come and gone and the traditional arguments were further undermined by skeptical objections by David Hume (1711-1776), Immanuel Kant (1724-1804), and Graham Oppy (1960-) among others. Yet the same response as stated previously can aid in safeguarding the validity of those arguments. Have the arguments themselves failed? If so, have they failed because of their formulation or because they have not been used presuppositionally to accomplish their aims in their areas of competence?[81] There lies the question of whether Pascal, and others by implication, have been justified in rejecting the traditional arguments.

Pascal's further objection against the use of reason and argument in apologetics lies in reason's inability to convert the hearer. Pascal states that conversion is the work of the Holy Spirit, but he does not address two significant related points. It appears that Pascal measures the utility of reason by persuasion itself, and if the argument given does not persuade the hearer then the argument is useless. One could think of reason and argument as performing a different role by *compelling* the hearer to greater conscious awareness and by implication greater consistency in their views. Reason and argument compel the hearer to either accept the conclusion of a sound argument because it is seen as sound, or it compels the hearer to provide a justification of

BLAISE PASCAL'S APOLOGETIC PROGRAM:

their disagreement. In either case reason calls the hearer to greater thoughtful engagement and commitment to his/her ideas—allowing reason to perform its function when properly used.

The second related topic is the role of reason in conversion—the work of the Holy Spirit and reason. Does the Holy Spirit work to convince, persuade, enlighten, and illuminate the mind by and with sound argument or above or apart from sound argument? That question while critical, it was not explored by Pascal. He affirms *that* salvation requires the work of the Holy Spirit (an indisputable claim), yet he does not explain *how* the Spirit accomplishes its end, neither what the role of reason is in the process.

Pascal's attempt to prove the impotence of reason led him to argue for the incomprehensible relation between the finite and the infinite. According to Pascal the infinite overwhelms the finite, it also makes the infinite paradoxically unattainable (greater knowledge does not yield proximity), and charges man with infinite hubris for seeking to understand the infinite. First, instead of arguing for a detrimental relation between the infinite and the finite, one can affirm that the infinite *includes*—by definition—the finite. It does not overwhelm it instead it accounts for the existence of the finite (a contingent being) and its intelligibility (the finite reveals the nature of the infinite).

Second, the suggested paradox is only possible when finite and infinite are conceived as quantitative measurements where the finite is only fulfilled when it apprehends the infinite in its fullness. Instead, why not argue for knowledge of the infinite as being an ultimate source of meaning that the finite can continue to understand to a greater and greater degree inexhaustibly, yet never undermining the real knowledge acquired by the finite in the process. Why could not the finite forever grow in true knowledge of God unendingly? Pascal makes a claim to the contrary but does not provide justification for his claim.

Third, Pascal answers his own claim by acknowledging that seeking to know God is not the product of pride in man but the necessary pursuit of our natures as rational: "Man is obviously made to think. It is his whole dignity and his whole merit; and his whole duty is to think as he ought."[82] It is part of our essence as humans to seek to understand the meaning and essential nature of things, as created, the essence of things reveal the nature of God, therefore it is the duty or fulfillment of human nature to know God's existence and nature. The knowledge of God as the good (chief end or *summum bonum*) is consistent with the purpose of man as stated in Genesis 1:28 (fill the earth and subdue it); Genesis 15:1 (I am your exceeding great reward); Psalm 27:4 (one thing I desire. . . to behold the beauty of the Lord); John 17:3 (eternal life is knowing God), among other passages of Scripture. Furthermore, man can only come to know God from knowledge of self towards the knowledge of God as stated by Pascal himself: "The order of thought is to begin with self, and with its author and its end."[83] Seeking to know God is not an act of hubris, but a fulfillment of our rational natures as made in the image of God (*imago dei*) for the sake of knowing God, making Him known, and therefore enjoying Him forever.

Pascal also charged reason with the futility of attaining any knowledge for to know anything requires knowledge of everything, and since knowledge of everything is an impossibility, then it follows that knowledge of anything is by implication an impossibility as well. While this argument at first encounter may appear cogent and persuasive, it passes by some important considerations with regards to knowledge. Knowledge of a being, relation, or state of being can be divided presuppositionaly on essential and nonessential or more basic and less basic. The basic/essential nature of things is accessible to the mind by concept formation through the use of reason to grasp the set of qualities that make a being, relation, or state of being what it is. One can understand foundational features of reality—like finite and infinite, changeable and unchangeable, matter and spirit, God and man, good and evil.

Less basic aspects of reality do not override foundational knowledge, on the contrary, what is foundational provides the basis to gradually understand what remains unknown that while complementing the more basic does not nullify or render meaningless. Pascal himself begins to lay ground for a response to his own challenge: "Since we cannot be universal and know all that is to be known of everything, we ought to know a little about everything."[84] Rather than a 'a little about everything', he should have said to know 'the basic things' about everything. Furthermore, if Pascal's original claim is to be applied consistently, then it would become a self-referentially absurd (SRA) claim for the finite cannot know everything and therefore all knowledge whatsoever would have been rendered impossible, and all distinctions and postulations equally meaningless—including special revelation.

Response to Arguments for Fideism

Men despise religion; they hate it and fear it is true. To remedy this, we must begin by showing that religion is not contrary to reason; that it is venerable, to inspire respect for it; then we must make it lovable, to make good men hope it is true; finally, we must prove it is true.[85]

The necessity for special revelation, embodied in the Scriptures, was a central project in Pascal's apologetical program. He sought to limit the excesses of rationalism in their denial of special revelation. In attempting to correct rationalism Pascal perhaps erred in the opposite direction by denying the clarity of general revelation—denying a foundational doctrine essential for the justification and intelligibility of the Gospel message. In the history of the church and in the Scriptures themselves, the belief in the clarity of general revelation served as the justification for the inexcusability of unbelief. Mankind is deserving of the judgement of God because we have failed to know and acknowledge God as the creator and upholder of the universe (breaking of the first commandment). The doctrine of the clarity of God's existence is expressed throughout Scripture and is identified by the apostle Paul at the beginning of his exposition of the gospel message in his letter to the Romans. In Romans 1:18-20 explain that mankind is inexcusable because the existence and nature of God have been clearly revealed since the creation of the world, being understood from the things that are made, so that men are without excuse for unbelief.

The clarity of God's existence in the creation and the moral law is corroborated throughout many passages of Scripture. The creation reveals the glory of God in its original state (Gen. 1:31), then God commanded Adam to uncover the revelation in the creation through the Dominion Mandate (Gen. 1:26-28), God's glory is declared in the created order (Ps. 8,19,104,111,150), the moral law is written in the hearts of men (Deut. 30:11-14 and Rom. 2:14-15), and the earth is full of the glory of God (Is. 6:3), in the history of the church, the clarity of general revelation are affirmed in the opening lines of the Westminster Confession of Faith (1643-1648)[86]and it is presupposed throughout it.

Pascal defended the revelation of God in Scripture at the expense and exclusion of the revelation of God in creation for he conceived of the world epistemically ambiguous and stated that God had deliberately left mankind in obscurity by not making His revelation clear in the creation.[87]Such claims represent a departure from key passages in Scripture and what has been affirmed in the historic Christian faith as summed up in creeds and councils. Pascal's move to deny the clarity of general revelation to affirm the necessity for Scripture has created an unnecessary conflict between the book of nature and redemptive revelation. To affirm the latter without justification from the former undermines the ability to show the veracity of Scripture. Which one of the claimed divine books is special revelation? That question was not addressed by Pascal, even though historically he would have been aware of the existence of the Quran. By what means is the question of inspiration of Scripture to be settled apart from the revelation of God in the creation? That is a question all the more relevant for modern apologists since awareness of other religions has increased in the modern world and a greater number of "divinely inspired books" have been proposed. It is my assessment that the denial of the clarity of general revelation represents the most significant shortcoming in Pascal's apologetical program. If one denies the clarity of general revelation, there is no basis for inexcusability, nor the means to justify the inspiration of Scripture among the several purported Scriptures.

Conclusion

Blaise Pascal's apologetical program represents the most significant challenge to the rationalist claims at the dawn of the Enlightenment. Pascal laid the ground in *Pensees* where he presented a series of arguments that are used by subsequent fideist thinkers in their desire to 'humble' reason's attempt to attain certainty in philosophy and religion. His program, in spite of its unsystematic layout, provides a comprehensive series of challenges against the use of reason in apologetics. Any serious attempt to address the relation of faith and reason, fideism and rationalism, religion and philosophy in the modern age must make careful use of Pascal's contributions to the discourse.

The brief response provided to Pascal's apologetic project marks the beginning of a still ongoing project.[88] If reason's place in philosophy, religion, and apologetics is to be properly addressed, then Pascal's challenges must be given careful attention and a comprehensive response that meets the exigencies of those challenges. In addition, the role of natural theology as a defense of the clarity of general revelation must likewise be given to deal with challenges to the faith that have become more acute after modernity.[89] Apologetics must fulfill its *offensive* role of taking all thoughts captive (II Cor. 10:4-5 and its *defensive* role of giving an account for the hope that is in us (1 Pet. 3:15).

Endnotes

[1]Frederick Copleston, *A History of Philosophy: Descartes to Leibniz, Volume IV.* (New York: A Doubleday Image Book, 1960), 153-154.

[2]Richard Popkin, *The History of Scepticism: From Savonarola to Bayle.* (New York: Oxford University Press, 2003), 143.

[3]*Ibid.,* 147.

[4]*Ibid.,* 151.

[5]*Ibid.,* 181.

[6]Encyclopaedia Britannica, inc., and Mortimer Jerome Adler.*The Great Books of the Western World.* (Chicago: Encyclopædia Britannica, 1994), Vol. 30, 186.

[7]Richard Popkin, *The History of Scepticism: From Savonarola to Bayle.* (New York: Oxford University Press, 2003), 181.

[8]Kenneth D. Boa & Robert M. Bowman Jr., *Faith Has Its Reasons: Integrative Approaches to Defending the Christian Faith.* (Downers Grove: Intervarsity Press, 2005), 342.

[9]Richard Popkin, *The History of Scepticism: From Savonarola to Bayle.* (New York: Oxford University Press, 2003), 181-184.

[10]Peter Kreeft. *Christianity for Modern Pagans: Pascal's Pensees, Edited, Outlined, and Explained.* (United States: Ignatius Press, 1993).

[11]Pascal's system has been the subject of much debate. Modern apologists have faced difficulties for Pascal's system does not fit within any of the majorly recognized apologetic schools of thought. He is not an evidentialist because he presupposes the existence of innate knowledge that precedes and is assumed in the interpretation of data. He is not a fideist/covenantal presuppositionalist because his justification for the veracity of Scripture consist in evidentialist proofs

from the fulfillment of prophecy. He is not a classical apologist for he denies the utility and soundness of the classical proofs—see Dr. Phil Fernandes' *The Apologetics Methodology of Blaise Pascal.*

[12]Rationalists have argued *against* the necessity of special revelation (Matthew Tindal, Lord Herbert of Cherbury) or have justified its need only *for the few* that lack intellectual abilities and training (John Locke), or have been unable to justify its existence (Lessing's "ugly broad ditch").

[13]Encyclopaedia Britannica, inc., and Mortimer Jerome Adler.*The Great Books of the Western World.* (Chicago: Encyclopædia Britannica, 1994, Vol. 30, 182.

[14]*Ibid.,* 184.

[15]Encyclopaedia Britannica, inc., and Mortimer Jerome Adler.*The Great Books of the Western World.* (Chicago: Encyclopædia Britannica, 1994), Vol. 30, 184.

[16]Plato and Aristotle both understood and postulated the good at the most foundational concept in ethics. It is the end in itself, the summum bonum, that which is chosen for its own sake, and is theologically spoken as the chief end of man.

[17]Encyclopaedia Britannica, inc., and Mortimer Jerome Adler.*The Great Books of the Western World.* (Chicago: Encyclopædia Britannica, 1994), Vol. 30, 185.

[18]*Ibid.,* 185.

[19]*Ibid.,* 186.

[20]*Ibid.,* 218.

[21]*Ibid.,* 217.

[22]*Ibid.,* 224.

[23]*Ibid.,* 185.

[24]*Ibid.,* 222.

[25]*Ibid.,* 183.

[26] *Ibid.,* 244.

[27]The futility of life apart from God "under the sun" is described by King Solomon in *Ecclesiastes.*

[28] *Ibid.*, 192.
[29] *Ibid.*, 249.
[30] *Ibid.*, 244.
[31] *Ibid.*, 301.
[32] *Ibid.*, 214.
[33] *Ibid.*, 246.
[34] *Ibid.*, 212.
[35] *Ibid.*, 240.
[36] *Ibid.*, 249-251.
[37] *Ibid.*, 224.
[38] *Ibid.*, 237.
[39] *Ibid.*,250.
[40] *Ibid.*, 182.
[41] *Ibid.*
[42] *Ibid.*, 184.
[43] *Ibid.*, 214.
[44] *Ibid.*, 183.
[45] *Ibid.*, 214.
[46] *Ibid.*, 222.
[47] *Ibid.*, 183.
[48] *Ibid.*, 223.
[49] *Ibid.*, 223.
[50] *Ibid.*, 223.
[51] *Ibid.*, 189
[52] *Ibid.*
[53] Richard Popkin, *The History of Scepticism: From Savonarola to Bayle.* (New York: Oxford University Press, 2003), 181.
[54] *Ibid.*, 181.
[55] *Ibid.*, xxi.
[56] *Ibid.*, 222.
[57] *Ibid.*, 222.
[58] *Ibid.*, 267.
[59] *Ibid.*, 266.

[60]*Ibid.*, 250.
[61]*Ibid.*, 250.
[62]*Ibid.*, 248-249.
[63]*Ibid.*, 249.
[64]*Ibid.*
[65]*Ibid.*, 225.
[66]*Ibid.*,224-225.   More specifically, Pascal lists 12 proofs that constitute 'The Proof " for Christianity: (1) Its establishment gently yet contrary to nature, (2) the sanctity of the Christian soul, (3) miracles, (4) Christ, (5) the Apostles, (6) Moses and the prophets, (7) the Jewish people, (8) the prophecies, (9) perpetuity, (10) the doctrine gives a reason for everything, (11) the sanctity of the law, and (12) the course of the world.
[67]*Ibid.*, 206.
[68]*Ibid.*, 213.
[69]*Ibid.*, 218.
[70]*Ibid.*
[71]*Ibid.*
[72]*Ibid.*, 205.
[73]*Ibid.*, 214.
[74]*Ibid.*, 215.
[75]*Ibid.*
[76]*Ibid.*, 216.
[77]*Ibid.*, 173.
[78]*Ibid.*, 171-172.
[79]*Ibid.*, 171.
[80]Surrendra Gangadean. *Philosophical Foundation: A Critical Analysis of Basic Beliefs*. (Lanhan: University Press of America, 2008), 62.
[81]A contemporary philosopher has sought to correct the perceived misuse of the classical arguments as well as reformulating them to overcome objections raised against them. Surrendra Gangadean's attempt has been formulated in his work: *Philosophical Foundation: A Critical Analysis of Basic Beliefs.*

[82] Encyclopaedia Britannica, inc., and Mortimer Jerome Adler. *The Great Books of the Western World*. (Chicago: Encyclopædia Britannica, 1994), Vol. 30, 200.

[83] *Ibid.*, 200.

[84] *Ibid.*, 177.

[85]*Ibid.*, 177.

[86]WCF 1:1 "Although the light of nature, and the works of creation and providence do so far manifest the goodness, wisdom, and power of God, as to leave men unexcusable; yet are they not sufficient to give that knowledge of God, and of His will, which is necessary unto salvation."

[87] Encyclopaedia Britannica, inc., and Mortimer Jerome Adler. *The Great Books of the Western World*. (Chicago: Encyclopædia Britannica, 1994), Vol. 30, 213, 245-247.

[88]Further work outlining the fideistic responses to the need for proof will be addressed in subsequent academic work in the near future.

[89]*Worldview pluralism*: there are so many worldviews, and the divisions within a worldview are many and longstanding. *Exclusivism*: affirmation of the absolute truth of the claims of Christianity. *Relativism*: in the name of tolerance the critical use of reason has been challenged when confronted with the virtue of tolerance. *Pragmatism*: has reduced the truth of religion to individual and collective utility divorced from truth claims. And *postmodern* deconstruction: denial of the universality of truth by reducing all worldviews and religions to interpretative meta-narrative frameworks of equal validity—See Owen Anderson, *The Clarity of God's Existence: The Ethics of Belief After the Enlightenment*. (Eugene: Wipf & Stock Pub. 2008).

CPSIA information can be obtained
at www.ICGtesting.com
Printed in the USA
FSHW010751220919
62265FS

9 780578 572543